I0050721

THE REGIONAL COMPREHENSIVE ECONOMIC PARTNERSHIP AGREEMENT

A NEW PARADIGM IN ASIAN REGIONAL COOPERATION?

MAY 2022

ADB

ASIAN DEVELOPMENT BANK

Creative Commons Attribution 3.0 IGO license (CC BY 3.0 IGO)

© 2022 Asian Development Bank
6 ADB Avenue, Mandaluyong City, 1550 Metro Manila, Philippines
Tel +63 2 8632 4444; Fax +63 2 8636 2444
www.adb.org

Some rights reserved. Published in 2022.

ISBN 978-92-9269-492-0 (print); 978-92-9269-493-7 (electronic); 978-92-9269-494-4 (ebook)
Publication Stock No. TCS220172-2
DOI: http://dx.doi.org/10.22617/TCS220172-2

The views expressed in this publication are those of the authors and do not necessarily reflect the views and policies of the Asian Development Bank (ADB) or its Board of Governors or the governments they represent.

ADB does not guarantee the accuracy of the data included in this publication and accepts no responsibility for any consequence of their use. The mention of specific companies or products of manufacturers does not imply that they are endorsed or recommended by ADB in preference to others of a similar nature that are not mentioned.

By making any designation of or reference to a particular territory or geographic area, or by using the term "country" in this document, ADB does not intend to make any judgments as to the legal or other status of any territory or area.

This work is available under the Creative Commons Attribution 3.0 IGO license (CC BY 3.0 IGO) https://creativecommons.org/licenses/by/3.0/igo/. By using the content of this publication, you agree to be bound by the terms of this license. For attribution, translations, adaptations, and permissions, please read the provisions and terms of use at https://www.adb.org/terms-use#openaccess.

This CC license does not apply to non-ADB copyright materials in this publication. If the material is attributed to another source, please contact the copyright owner or publisher of that source for permission to reproduce it. ADB cannot be held liable for any claims that arise as a result of your use of the material.

Please contact pubsmarketing@adb.org if you have questions or comments with respect to content, or if you wish to obtain copyright permission for your intended use that does not fall within these terms, or for permission to use the ADB logo.

Corrigenda to ADB publications may be found at http://www.adb.org/publications/corrigenda.

Notes:
In this publication, "$" refers to United States dollars.
ADB recognizes "China" as the People's Republic of China, "Korea" as the Republic of Korea, and "Vietnam" as Viet Nam.

Cover design by Jasper Lauzon. On the cover: major port systems, vegetable market, and consultation photos by Ariel Javellana; airport and shopping mall photos by Lester Ledesma; public market and face mask vendor photos by Chor Sokunthea; ship photo by Abir Abdullah; fish port photo by Raymond Panaligan; and field worker photo by Ian Taylor.

Contents

Tables, Figures, and Boxes

Tables

Figures

Boxes

Foreword

With Asia intent on staying on the path of economic recovery in 2022, the Regional Comprehensive Economic Partnership (RCEP) can be a timely tool to foster regional integration and economic growth. RCEP, partnering Southeast Asian nations with Australia, the People's Republic of China, Japan, New Zealand, and the Republic of Korea, has the potential to strengthen manufacturing supply chains, raise productivity, and increase wages and employment.

RCEP was conceptualized in November 2012 to attain a comprehensive and mutually beneficial economic partnership agreement. After 8 years of negotiations, RCEP was signed on 15 November 2020. This laid a historic milestone on the road toward deeper economic integration. RCEP entered into force on 1 January 2022. It is nevertheless not the time to relax efforts. RCEP does not supersede existing free trade agreements and expected gains will not be automatic. RCEP will be closely watched to see whether it delivers on greater liberalization and economic cooperation.

To support member economies' efforts to overcome implementation challenges, this report analyses and compares the legal text of RCEP, the Comprehensive and Progressive Agreement for Trans-Pacific Partnership (CPTPP), and with relevant agreements of the World Trade Organization. The report covers all RCEP chapters—including trade in goods; ROO; sanitary and phytosanitary measures; technical barriers to trade; trade in services; investment; movement of people; and cross-cutting issues of intellectual property, small enterprises, and e-commerce, among others. Its analysis helps provide a better understanding of RCEP's potential for benefits and value added over existing agreements around traditional issues of trade and investment liberalization and newer issues of regulatory coherence in building a better environment for business. It is hoped that the report can serve as a valuable resource to support policy makers and negotiators in RCEP implementation by identifying areas where further work is needed to make the agreement more attractive to final users, namely firms and investors.

The report shows RCEP presents valuable opportunities to deepen regional economic integration. Critically important are the agreement's built-in provisions and economic and technical cooperation measures that make it possible to expand RCEP's depth and coverage in the future. To realize this potential, policy makers and economic actors will need to forge appropriate responses to navigate the development and implementation challenges of the agenda. The report offers policy recommendations that can generate bold ideas for effective strategies to unlock new opportunities and orient RCEP toward successful implementation.

The Asian Development Bank continues to work closely with RCEP stakeholders to ensure effective implementation and evolution of the agreement toward strengthening regional integration and supporting inclusive and sustainable growth.

Albert Park
Chief Economist and Director General
Economic Research and Regional Cooperation Department
Asian Development Bank

Acknowledgments

This publication was prepared by the Regional Cooperation and Integration Division (ERCI) of the Economic Research and Regional Cooperation Department (ERCD), Asian Development Bank (ADB). It was financed by ADB under the Knowledge and Support Technical Assistance (TA) 6740: Raising the Value of Regional Trade Agreements—Key Factors for Successful Implementation and Positive Economic Impact, with funding support from ADB's Technical Assistance Special Fund (TASF-7 and TASF-Others) and the Regional Cooperation and Integration Fund.

Cyn-Young Park, ERCI Director provided overall direction and supervision of the report at ADB.

Francesco Abbate (ADB consultant) and Pramila A. Crivelli, Economist in ERCI, are the lead authors of this report covering all the Regional Comprehensive Economic Partnership (RCEP) chapters and schedule of tariff commitments. Sanchita Basu Das, Economist in ERCI, drafted elements of the section on origin and rationale of the RCEP agreement and contributed to the sections on regulatory issues. Stefano Inama (United Nations Conference on Trade and Development [UNCTAD]) provided inputs as well as guidance on the review, interpretation, and comparison of the legal text of the trade agreements. Mark Pearson (ADB consultant), Pramila A. Crivelli, and Stefano Inama worked on the codification and analysis of product-specific rules of origin. Thi Hang Banh (ADB consultant) provided valuable assistance in compiling and analyzing RCEP tariff commitments.

The publication also benefited from the valuable insights from the ERCD Office of the Chief Economist and Director General and ADB regional departments during the review process. We are most grateful for their feedback and advice.

The publication was produced with the support of many members within ADB. Pramila A. Crivelli, Sanchita Basu Das, and Paulo Rodelio Halili, Senior Economics Officer in ERCI, conducted the groundwork, and coordinated overall production. James Unwin edited the manuscript. Jasper Lauzon created the cover design. Mike Cortes did the layout and typesetting. Cherry Lynn Zafaralla performed proofreading, while Marjorie Celis did the page proof checking, with support from Paulo Rodelio Halili, Carol Ongchangco (Operations Coordinator), and Gerald Pascua. Support for printing and publishing this report was provided by the Printing Services Unit of ADB's Corporate Services Department and by the publishing team of the Department of Communications.

Abbreviations

AANZFTA	–	ASEAN–Australia–New Zealand Free Trade Agreement
ACIA	–	ASEAN Comprehensive Investment Agreement
ADB	–	Asian Development Bank
AEC	–	ASEAN Economic Community
AFTA	–	ASEAN free trade area
ASEAN	–	Association of Southeast Asian Nations
ATIGA	–	ASEAN Trade in Goods Agreement
COVID–19	–	coronavirus disease
CPTPP	–	Comprehensive and Progressive Agreement for Trans-Pacific Partnership
CTH	–	change of tariff heading
DEA	–	Digital Economy Agreement
DEPA	–	Digital Economy Partnership Agreement
FTA	–	free trade agreement
GPA	–	government procurement agreement
IPR	–	intellectual property rights
JSI	–	Joint Statement Initiative on E-commerce
MFN	–	most-favored nation
NTM	–	nontariff measure
OECD	–	Organisation for Economic Co-operation and Development
PRC	–	People's Republic of China
PSROs	–	product-specific rules of origin
RCEP	–	regional Comprehensive Economic Partnership
ROO	–	rules of origin
RVC	–	Regional value content
SMEs	–	small and medium-sized enterprises
SOE	–	state-owned enterprise
SPS	–	sanitary and phytosanitary measures
TBT	–	technical barriers to trade
TFA	–	trade facilitation agreement
TPP	–	Trans-Pacific Partnership
TRIMS	–	trade-related investment measures
TRIPS	–	trade-related aspects of intellectual property rights
UNCTAD	–	United Nations Conference on Trade and Development
WTO	–	World Trade Organization

Executive Summary

Regional Comprehensive Economic Partnership: Origin and Rationale

The Regional Comprehensive Economic Partnership (RCEP) is a milestone achievement in regional economic integration, led by the Association of Southeast Asian Nations (ASEAN) over the last 3 decades. Since the initial ASEAN Free Trade Area agreement was signed in 1992, ASEAN has expanded its membership and undertaken a more comprehensive form of integration in 2003 toward the creation of the ASEAN Economic Community (AEC) in 2015. ASEAN has adopted the AEC Blueprint 2025 to deepen the regional integration process by 2025. AEC covered many initiatives at two levels: within ASEAN members and between ASEAN and the external partners. ASEAN signed six free trade agreements with external partners, including Australia-New Zealand; the People's Republic of China (PRC); Hong Kong, China; India; Japan; and the Republic of Korea.

Despite its efforts, ASEAN has often been criticized for creating a "noodle bowl" effect from multiple free trade agreements (FTAs) in the region, raising costs, and negating the benefits of these trade deals. RCEP was formed to mitigate challenges faced by businesses across multiple FTAs. It was developed as a comprehensive agreement, covering issues of market access, regulatory coherence across trade in goods and services, investment and other cross-sectoral issues such as intellectual property rights, competition policy, government procurement, electronic commerce, support for small and medium-sized enterprises (SMEs), and others. RCEP helped ASEAN to entrench its centrality, strengthening its function as a hub in the wider trade architecture of Asia and the Pacific.

The RCEP is often compared to another megaregional agreement, the Comprehensive and Progressive Agreement for Trans-Pacific Partnership (CPTPP). Though both have similar objectives to promote trade and investment in a mutually beneficial manner, CPTPP is applauded for its wider scope and depth. RCEP is touted to be accommodative in its ambition paying attention to the development differences of the member economies. RCEP will be closely watched to see whether it can resolve many of the past challenges with multiple FTAs in the region and deliver on greater liberalization and economic cooperation.

This report provides a preliminary analysis of the legal text in RCEP, comparing it with that of the CPTPP, relevant agreements of the World Trade Organization (WTO), and ASEAN+1 FTAs, taking into account related literature articulating potential economic impacts. RCEP follows the "ASEAN way"[1] of consultation and consensus to manage regional trade integration through a combined agenda of implementation and built-in provisions for making gradual progress in trade liberalization, rather than firm commitments adopted at the outset and contained in the original text, as was the case for CPTPP. The report ends with a mix of policy recommendations and suggests road maps to orient RCEP toward successful implementation.

---

[1] The "ASEAN way" is a way of making decisions among ASEAN countries, i.e., *musyawarah* (discussion and consultation), *mufakat* (unanimous decision), and consensus.

This report is divided into six parts and 19 chapters, covering all key provisions of the RCEP trade agreement. Each of the 19 chapters in this study outlines the scope and objective and provides a preliminary assessment of the legal text. The chapters also compare RCEP commitments to those of CPTPP and WTO, as necessary. This report concludes with discussion on the way forward.

Trade in Goods

Market access for trade in goods (i.e., preferential tariffs) is the traditional form of trade liberalization, and still covers a significant part of an FTA. RCEP is widely expected to bring significant benefits in this area by providing a common instrument that may, on one hand, gradually overlap with the panoply of existing FTAs and, on the other, provide a preferential platform for countries not previously engaged in an FTA (e.g., the PRC and Japan). The preliminary analysis of the structure (38 tariff offers) and the phaseout periods (in some cases over 20 years) of the tariff offers provides sobering expectations.

The absence of a most-favored nation (MFN) provision for the inclusion of the tariff liberalizations existing in other FTAs is a sign that RCEP will coexist with the ASEAN Trade in Goods Agreement (ATIGA) and ASEAN+1 FTAs2 and other bilateral FTAs). Many RCEP countries have presented differentiated offers. Some ASEAN countries have made differentiated offers even toward other ASEAN members. The introduction of tariff differentials and related provisions have brought another layer of complexity to implementing tariff reductions. Additional insights from detailed analysis of tariff offers from Cambodia, Japan, and Viet Nam, taken as a sample, reveal long phasing-out periods for many tariff lines and complete exclusion from tariff liberalization for others, potentially affecting the value of such offers in terms of competitive market access.

Rules of Origin

Rules of origin (ROO) and related administrative procedures are another cornerstone of preferential market access. Given the existing complexity and overlapping of ROO in ASEAN FTAs, RCEP has been welcomed as a game changer, thanks to the possibility to (i) cumulate inputs within the whole RCEP region to qualify as a RCEP originating product, and (ii) to bring under a single FTA the thousands of product-specific rules of origin (PSROs) scattered across many ASEAN FTAs.

This report points out that the agreement is yet to completely match the expectations. A firm would use the FTA that is providing the best combination in tariff offer and ROO. Furthermore, the kind of cumulation provided under RCEP is limited to cumulation of inputs originating in other RCEP countries but not to working or processing carried out in other RCEP countries and subject to the application of tariff differentials.

In simple words, a product manufactured in Cambodia using inputs from the PRC and exported to the Republic of Korea may be considered a product of the PRC instead of a Cambodian product with the consequent application of a less generous tariff schedule unless the provisions for tariff differentials are met. Last but not least, RCEP text on administration of the proof of origin (the so-called Certificate of Origin) does not provide for self-certification but still relies, though with some flexibility, on the use of certificates of origin stamped with official seals and signatures of the certifying authorities.

Sanitary and Phytosanitary Measures and Technical Barriers to Trade

Recent studies show a rise of nontariff measures (NTMs) in Asia. NTMs related to requirements on sanitary and phytosanitary measures (SPS) and technical barriers to trade (TBT) are among the most widely used. The detailed analysis conducted in this report—comparing key WTO provisions and elements regulating TBT and SPS in FTAs with those contained in the respective SPS and TBT chapters of RCEP and CPTPP—could not identify any WTO-plus provision in RCEP and highlights the reduced coverage of such key commitments compared to those contained in CPTPP. RCEP provisions on SPS and TBT therefore need to be strengthened to offer a common platform and facilitate the elimination of NTMs. An SPS or a TBT committee serving as a forum where experts in such highly technical disciplines could meet to bring forward the agenda could help progress towards this goal. Unlike for CPTPP, RCEP does not provide for the establishment of such a committee.

Trade Remedies

An initial analysis conducted in this report shows that RCEP countries are increasingly using trade remedies against RCEP partners. Chapter 7 – Trade Remedies of the RCEP Agreement does not show, as in CPTPP, any significant WTO-plus provision, and contains a series of procedural guarantees for on-the-spot investigation, notification, and consultation, such as those usually included in FTAs. The most relevant aspect of this chapter is the overwhelming importance given to safeguard measures during the transitional period when tariff offers are implemented. Compared with the CPTPP text, the relevant provisions and the overall drafting of the transitional RCEP safeguard measures appear to leave more discretion to the investigating authorities and member states on the application and duration of these measures, which may impact the effective implementation and predictability of the tariff concessions.

Customs Procedures and Trade Facilitation

This chapter covers much the same areas as those in WTO's Trade Facilitation Agreement (TFA) and CPTPP. RCEP is ahead of WTO and CPTPP in this area of commitment. RCEP nevertheless appears ahead of WTO and CPTPP in this area of commitments. RCEP goes farther than TFA's ambitions in two WTO-plus topics albeit using hortatory language. One, RCEP calls for customs clearance of goods within 48 hours of arrival. For express consignments, the time limit is reduced to 6 hours. Two, RCEP contains improved advance ruling provisions and a time limit of 150 days for the issuance of advance rulings. RCEP also contains two "CPTPP-plus" provisions: a 6-hour limit on customs clearance of perishable goods, and an option for member countries to take longer to fully implement their commitments. This could have a greater impact on trade liberalization and strengthening global value chains than tariff reductions alone.

Trade in Services, Including Financial and Professional Services, and Telecommunications

RCEP advances the coverage of commitments in this area, while the cautious approach remains. The scope and structure of Chapter 8 – Trade in Services of the Regional Comprehensive Economic Partnership Agreement essentially replicate those in the more recent ASEAN+1 FTAs and CPTPP. RCEP will not result, as expected by some observers, in a single, user-friendly set of rules for the whole region because its MFN provision does not extend the benefits of previous market access concessions by a Party to the other Parties. Therefore, RCEP rules may be intensifying the "noodle bowl" effect created by

30 PTAs that have already been signed or are in force between RCEP members and by the participation of most of them in either CPTPP or FTAs with non-CPTPP members, or both.

However, RCEP appears to cover a greater share of overall trade in services between member countries. That is a result of the groundbreaking adoption of negative list schedules by all members—though with different timelines—and increased market access in specific sectors. New market access opportunities have been identified in a variety of sectors, including educational services, health services, computer-related services, and other business services, in such countries as the PRC, Indonesia, the Philippines, and Thailand. However, a deep comparative analysis of schedules of commitments and non-conforming measures is yet to be conducted. Furthermore, bearing in mind the history of ASEAN trade in the services agenda, it remains to be seen whether the RCEP built-in provisions for further liberalization will run to schedule, leading to effective services liberalization.

The RCEP Chapter 8 also provides three specific annexes on financial services, telecommunications, and professional services, with commitments and frameworks for enhanced cooperation. On financial services, compared to ASEAN+1 FTAs, the incremental value is constituted by higher foreign equity caps in some commitments and coverage of "new financial services". On telecommunications, RCEP's value added results from (i) coverage of mobile services, including number portability and provisions on flexibility in the choice of technology; and (ii) new market access opportunities stemming from the commitments made by Indonesia, the Lao People's Democratic Republic (Lao PDR), Malaysia, and Thailand. With regard to professional services, the PRC has made new commitments—resulting in greater market access for firms supplying legal, architectural, planning, engineering, veterinary, accounting, auditing, and bookkeeping services.

Movement of Natural Persons

The RCEP under Chapter 9 – Temporary Movement of Natural Persons (MNP) appears to be more liberal than CPTPP. The MNP provisions aim to be more liberal than CPTPP. It aims to facilitate movement of people on temporary basis engaged in trade in goods, supply of services or conduct of investment. This will occur by ensuring efficient visa-processing procedures and transparency-related requirements in processing applications. Coverage of RCEP Chapter 9 is limited to business visitors, intra-corporate transferees, or persons specified in the members' schedule contained in RCEP Annex IV.

The rules included in this chapter are almost the same as those governing MNP in the ASEAN–Australia–New Zealand FTA (AANZFTA) and other ASEAN+1 FTAs.

Investment

The value added of RCEP Chapter 10 – Investment on enhanced investment liberalization and protection is likely to be small, due to factors that include RCEP investors already being covered through many international investment agreements and FTAs with investment provisions that member countries are part of. Moreover, state–state dispute settlement mechanisms can be cumbersome and politically sensitive (UNCTAD 2017). Therefore, the absence of investor–state dispute settlement in RCEP is likely to cause investors to make use of investor–state dispute settlement in existing FTAs and international investment agreements.

The chapter includes several positive features:

(i) All member countries have adopted a negative list approach on entry into force, although the list of exemptions in coverage is long and affects many sectors.

(ii) The "Trade-Related Investment Measures (TRIMs)-plus" prohibition of performance requirements is extended to forced transfer of a particular technology, production process, or other proprietary knowledge, as well as forced adoption of a given rate or amount of royalty under a license contract.

(iii) Greater market access results, mainly from the alignment of RCEP commitments with those under CPTPP.

Intellectual Property

Chapter 11 – Intellectual Property of the RCEP Agreement can be regarded as a quantum leap from the relatively subdued treatment of this subject in ASEAN FTAs. It covers, although with widely varying degrees of detail, the standard set of areas enshrined in the Trade-Related Aspects of Intellectual Property Rights (TRIPS) Agreement as well as a new field: genetic resources, traditional knowledge, and folklore.

The most distinct feature of RECP's discipline on intellectual property is its emphasis to reconcile *"the rights of intellectual property right holders and the legitimate interests of users and the public interest".*[2] As a result, the "fair use" exception has been extended to include not only copyright but also trademarks, thus constituting a "CPTPP-plus" of the chapter. Furthermore, with regard to Geographical Indications, member countries can challenge the protection of a name as a Geographical Indication in another Party, if consumers in the member country concerned know the name as the common descriptive term for the good in question. In such case, producers of those goods will not be prevented from using what is considered as a common name.

The value added of the intellectual property provisions would vary from country to country. It would be marginal for the seven RCEP countries that are also CPTPP members (Australia, Brunei Darussalam, Japan, Malaysia, New Zealand, Singapore, and Viet Nam). However, as trading partners they would benefit from eventual improvement in the intellectual property regimes of the remaining eight countries. In principle, the least developed countries should be the major beneficiaries, provided that their legislation and enforcement are upgraded so as to meet the RCEP requirements. For the PRC, RCEP is expected to have some positive, though limited, effects on intellectual property protection. What is probably more interesting is how RCEP will impact enforcement of the revised or new intellectual property laws in the PRC and the further alignment of intellectual property protection at the regional level.

Electronic Commerce

The provisions in RCEP Chapter 12 – Electronic Commerce have been heavily influenced by those originally embodied into the original Trans-Pacific Partnership (TPP) and then reproduced, with no changes, in CPTPP. According to many observers, e-commerce and other digital trade-related rules were *"the most transformative measures"* in the whole TPP (United States International Trade Commission 2016, p. 353). Most provisions are similar or identical across RCEP and CPTPP. However, provisions on data flows and data localization, which firms providing

---

[2] Article 11.1.1 (c) of "Objectives" in RCEP Chapter 11 – Intellectual Property.

computer services consider to be fundamental, are less stringent in RCEP, which allows for more policy space.

Nevertheless, these commitments are the first of a kind for non-CPTPP members, as they go beyond those in FTAs between RCEP countries and the ASEAN Agreement on Electronic Commerce. In RCEP, the countries have agreed for the free flows of data and no forced data localization as a default measure. The broad exceptions provision though limit the potential of these commitments.

Another interesting feature of RCEP Chapter 12 is the Dialogue on Electronic Commerce, a forum for member countries to discuss topics such as cooperation; current and emerging issues; and matters relevant to the development and use of electronic commerce.

Competition

The provisions in RCEP Chapter 13 – Competition reflect growing awareness among member countries of the importance of competition law and policy and recognition of the significant differences in the capacity and governance of RCEP countries. Recent progress in national legislations has translated into much deeper competition law and policy provisions in RCEP than those in ASEAN+1 FTAs.

Member countries are required to adopt or maintain competition laws and regulations that prohibit anticompetitive activities and to establish or maintain authorities to implement its competition laws. Each member country is also obliged to apply its competition laws and regulations to all entities engaged in commercial activities, including state-owned enterprises (SOEs). However, the chapter recognizes the sovereign rights of each participating nation to develop and enforce its own competition laws and policies, allowing for exclusion or exemptions based on the grounds of public policy or public interest.

While RCEP and CPTPP share many similarities in the competition law and policy field, they diverge in a number of major ways. CPTPP devotes a separate chapter to SOEs, unlike RCEP, which contains no specific provisions on them. The absence of an RCEP commitment on the private right of action constitutes one of the most conspicuous differences. More generally, CPTPP's provisions are much deeper, involving obligations in other critical areas, such as procedural fairness in competition law enforcement and transparency.

Small and Medium-Sized Enterprises

Building on CPTP's example, RCEP is the first FTA involving all ASEAN countries that includes a separate chapter on SMEs. The objective of Chapter 14 – Small and Medium Enterprises of the RCEP Agreement is *"to promote information sharing and cooperation in increasing the ability of SMEs to utilize and benefit from the opportunities created by this Agreement.[3]"* In addition, other chapters in the Agreement address SME issues, such as those dealing with electronic commerce and customs and trade facilitation. However, key benefits accruing to SMEs are expected to come from lowered tariff and nontariff barriers, increased market access for service providers, and trade facilitation rather than the very chapter devoted to SMEs.

---

[5]   Article 14.1.1 of "Objectives" in RCEP Chapter 14 – Small and Medium Enterprises.

Economic and Technical Cooperation

Participating countries are requested to undertake economic and technical cooperation activities, which are trade- or investment-related, including capacity building and technical assistance that focus on (i) trade in goods; (ii) trade in services; (iii) investment; (iv) intellectual property; (v) electronic commerce; (vi) competition; and (vii) SMEs. RCEP Chapter 15 – Economic and Technical Cooperation calls for a work program to be developed under the Committee on Sustainable Development, taking into account the needs identified in various RCEP committees. This report formulates a number of proposals in this area.

Government Procurement

The provisions contained in Chapter 16 – Government Procurement are the shortest and most modest, in both scope and depth, in the whole RCEP Agreement. The provisions only apply to procurement implemented by central government entities, thus excluding subnational government bodies and state-owned enterprises. It only includes procurement that is *"expressly open to international competition"* and is aligned with generally accepted government procurement principles.[4] The focus of the chapter is largely limited to transparency and cooperation. However, this is the first time when rules on government procurement have been introduced to seven RCEP members that have neither joined CPTPP nor WTO's Government Procurement Agreement. These are Cambodia, the PRC, Indonesia, the Lao PDR, Myanmar, the Philippines, and Thailand.

Procurement provisions in RCEP and CPTPP are very similar, although CPTPP is more up-to-date and includes build-operate-transfer (BOT) contracts. Furthermore, in contrast to CPTPP, RCEP contains no provisions regarding international labor rights, reflecting the reservations of several RCEP developing countries on this issue.

Implementation and Built-in Agenda: Challenges and Policy Implications

Implementation

Full and timely implementation of the RCEP Agreement is the key ingredient for its success. RCEP requires six ASEAN members and three non-ASEAN countries to ratify the Agreement before it becomes effective. As of 15 December 2021, six ASEAN members (Brunei Darussalam, Cambodia, the Lao PDR, Singapore, Thailand, and Viet Nam) and five non-ASEAN countries (Australia, the PRC, Japan, the Republic of Korea, and New Zealand) had ratified the Agreement.. Hence, RCEP entered into force on 1 January 2022 in the first 10 signatory countries, and on 1 February 2022 in the Republic of Korea.

As experience has widely demonstrated, leadership of RCEP members in this endeavor is the most important factor. While the Agreement text provides for the establishment of a secretariat, its role and resources are yet to be clearly delineated.

---

4   Article 16.3 of "Principles" in RCEP Chapter 16 – Government Procurement.

The RCEP's implementation implies (i) individual member countries carrying out their commitments; and (ii) institutional action for the execution of general provisions, including those that are part of the built-in agenda. This report stresses the challenges associated with implementation by individual member countries, especially with regard to key chapters such as trade in goods, covering tariff offers; ROO; customs procedures, which significantly affect trade costs; trade in services, involving the switch by eight members from the positive to the negative list; investment; intellectual property; and competition.

The RCEP secretariat or an independent institution should closely monitor the implementation of tariff offers. A dedicated website should be established to provide information about how to benefit from RCEP, by listing in a user-friendly manner the tariff offers and related ROO. Limited awareness is one of the many causes for low utilization of preferential rates in the ASEAN Free Trade Area (AFTA) tariff scheme. RCEP should address these issues from the beginning and institutionalize a practice that would make RCEP's utilization rates publicly available.

The key aspect of implementation within member countries is the dissemination of information on the results of the Agreement and its new opportunities for trade and investment for all stakeholders, particularly SMEs. The key aspect of implementation within member countries is the dissemination of information on the results of the Agreement and its new opportunities for trade and investment for all stakeholders, particularly SMEs. In the past, ASEAN has faced some challenges in this area. This report thus suggests that besides having a regionwide website, the Committee on Sustainable Development should promote each member country having a website to provide SME users with easily accessible information on RCEP and ways to use it to their advantage.

It is well known that procedures are generally more complex and time-consuming for the implementation of nontariff provisions, as a new or amended law is followed by rules and regulations. The report highlights the special needs of least developed countries and other lower middle-income countries in their implementation processes. Close monitoring of implementation by all members should be among the main responsibilities of the RCEP Joint Committee, consisting of senior officials designated by each member countries, with assistance from the RCEP secretariat.

In the area of electronic commerce, this report puts forward another proposal concerning institutional actions. The Dialogue on Electronic Commerce, to be established within the RCEP Joint Committee, should contribute to (i) forging a common position among RCEP members within WTO's Joint Statement Initiative on E-commerce (JSI); and (ii) building convergence on social issues (inclusion, SMEs, internet access, a safe online environment) and advanced topics in digital innovation, such as artificial intelligence and financial technology or fintech.

A special initiative should be arranged for SPS and TBTs to make up for the absence of a joint committee to pursue further regional action. This could take the form of an intergovernmental body using the existing RCEP committee or it could be a new ad hoc mechanism.

Built-in Agenda

The RCEP contains several provisions that could lead to further negotiations. In many cases, these provisions relate to pending issues that have not been agreed upon during negotiations. On some of such commitments, this report advances a number of proposals, including the following:

(i) **Trade in goods**. With regard to tariffs, further analysis should be carried out to clearly identify the areas and sectors where further negotiations are needed to make RCEP more competitive than the network of existing FTAs. These studies should be triggering the activation of Article 2.5: Acceleration of Tariff Commitments, and Article 2.21: Sectoral Initiatives to achieve greater and faster tariff liberalization.

(ii) **Rules of origin**. A research and capacity building program should be carried out to formulate proposals for the implementation of the built-in agenda on cumulation and proof of origin.

Furthermore, this report offers policy recommendations that could result in future negotiations for the following RCEP chapters that do not include any built-in agenda at present:

(i) **Customs procedures.** The Committee on Goods should (a) mandate members to use a single entry point and to employ World Customs Organization standards by a given deadline, and (b) introduce de minimis rules, allowing imports below a given monetary value to enter member countries duty-free.

(ii) **Temporary entry of natural persons.** As with CPTPP, this report proposes establishment of Committee on Temporary Entry for Business Persons to (a) review the implementation and operation of RCEP Chapter 9, and (b) consider opportunities for the Parties to further facilitate the temporary entry of business persons.

In all these areas of possible negotiations, the lower-middle-income countries, especially the least developed countries, would greatly benefit from technical cooperation and capacity building in order to become more active in such negotiations .

Part I
Introduction

1. Regional Comprehensive Economic Partnership: Origin and Rationale

The Regional Comprehensive Economic Partnership (RCEP) has often been defined as the natural corollary of the efforts of the Association of Southeast Asian Nations (ASEAN) to strengthen regional integration efforts within ASEAN members—Brunei Darussalam, Cambodia, Indonesia, the Lao People's Democratic Republic (Lao PDR), Malaysia, Myanmar, the Philippines, Singapore, Thailand, and Viet Nam—and with external partners. ASEAN countries have consistently taken interest in developing intraregional integration and advanced it from an ASEAN Free Trade Area (AFTA) in the 1990s to a more comprehensive form of integration in 2003, called the ASEAN Economic Community (AEC). ASEAN established the AEC in 2015 and adopted the AEC Blueprint 2025 to further deepen regional integration measures by 2025. Simultaneously, ASEAN has extended its integration initiative to nonmembers and progressively built a network of free trade agreements (FTAs) with Dialogue Partners:[1] Australia and New Zealand; the People's Republic of China (PRC); India; Japan; the Republic of Korea; and Hong Kong, China.

The RCEP was signed on 15 November 2020, when ASEAN's 10 members and 5 of its free trade area (FTA) partners—Australia, the PRC, Japan, the Republic of Korea, and New Zealand—agreed to work together under a single umbrella of economic cooperation. The formation of RCEP was viewed by many as pathbreaking for ASEAN as not only did it establish ASEAN's centrality[2] in leading the economic cooperation architecture in Asia and the Pacific, RCEP signaled an attempt to resolve the "noodle bowl" effect of the array of FTAs that proliferated in the region over the previous 2 decades (Table 1). By 2021, RCEP gained recognition as a trade arrangement able to help revive international trade and economic development as the spread of the coronavirus disease (COVID-19) pandemic highlighted the downside of globalization and supply chains.

The RCEP entered into force on 1 January 2022.[3] The agreement had required RCEP to come into practice 60 days after the date at which the minimum number of ratification notification is achieved—i.e., six ASEAN members and three non-ASEAN countries. As of 15 December 2021, six ASEAN members (Brunei Darussalam, Cambodia, the Lao PDR, Singapore, Thailand, and Viet Nam) and five non-ASEAN countries (Australia, the PRC, Japan, the Republic of Korea, and New Zealand) had ratified the Agreement.[4]

---

[1] ASEAN conducts its external relationship through dialogue cooperation and partnership. It deepens its relation by conferring formal status of Dialogue Partners, Sectoral Dialogue Partners, and Development Partners. Of the 11 ASEAN Dialogue Partners, ASEAN had signed free trade agreements with six of them. Australia-New Zealand was treated as one based on their existing cooperation arrangement called Closer Economic Relations (CER) cooperation agreement.

[2] ASEAN Centrality assumes that ASEAN, instead of the bigger economies should be the hub of developing a wider regional architecture in Asia and the Pacific.

[3] Association of Southeast Asian Nations. 2021. Regional Comprehensive Economic Partnership (RCEP) Agreement to Enter into Force on 1 January 2022. News release. 21 November. https://asean.org/regional-comprehensive-economic-partnership-rcep-to-enter-into-force-on-1-january-2022/.

[4] The RCEP entered into force on 1 January 2022 in the first 10 signatory countries, and on 1 February 2022 in the Republic of Korea.

Table 1: Current FTAs among RCEP Members and Year of Entry into Force

Economies/ Regions		RCEP					
		ASEAN	Australia	PRC	Japan	New Zealand	Korea, Rep. of
RCEP	ASEAN		AANZFTA, 2010 Singapore, 2003 Thailand, 2005 Malaysia, 2013 CPTPP, 2018 Indonesia, 2020	ASEAN, 2005 Thailand, 2003 Singapore, 2009 Cambodia, (2022)	ASEAN, 2008 Singapore, 2002 Brunei Darussalam, 2008 Indonesia, 2008 Malaysia, 2006 Thailand, 2007 Philippines, 2008 Viet Nam, 2009 CPTPP, 2018	AANZFTA, 2010 Thailand, 2005 Malaysia, 2010 CPTPP, 2018 Singapore, 2001 TPSEP/P4, 2006 DEPA, 2021	ASEAN, 2007 Singapore, 2006 Viet Nam, 2015 Philippines*
	Australia			2015	Bilateral, 2015 CPTPP, 2018	CER, 1983 CPTPP, 2018 AANZFTA, 2010 PACER Plus, 2020	2014
	PRC				No FTA	2008 CPTPP, 2018	2015 No FTA
	Japan						
	NZ						2015
	Korea, Republic of						

AANZFTA = ASEAN–Australia–New Zealand FTA; ASEAN = Association of Southeast Asian Nations; CER = Australia–New Zealand Closer Economic Relations Trade Agreement; CPTPP = Comprehensive and Progressive Agreement for Trans-Pacific Partnership; DEPA = Digital Economy Partnership Agreement (Chile, New Zealand, and Singapore); FTA = free trade agreement; NZ = New Zealand; PACER Plus = Pacific Agreement on Closer Economic Relations; PRC = People's Republic of China; TPSEP/P4 = Trans-Pacific Strategic Economic Partnership Agreement.
* Concluded negotiations in October 2021.
Source: Crivelli and Inama (2022a).

The RCEP was conceptualized in November 2012, based on a framework endorsed during the ASEAN Summit in November 2011.[5] It was to built on discussion of two other regional cooperation arrangements, the East Asia Free Trade Agreement and the Comprehensive Economic Partnership in East Asia initiative, which worked on either ASEAN+3 or ASEAN+6 membership configuration. RCEP was not designed to work on a predetermined membership. Rather, it was formed on the basis of open accession that enabled participation of any of the ASEAN FTA partners at the outset or later when they were ready to join. The arrangement was kept open to any other external economic partners (Basu Das 2015b).

[5] ASEAN. 2012. *Guiding Principles and Objectives for Negotiating the Regional Comprehensive Economic Partnership.* https://asean.org/wp-content/uploads/2012/05/RCEP-Guiding-Principles-public-copy.pdf.

From the beginning, RCEP's objective was to attain a comprehensive and mutually beneficial economic partnership agreement that was expected to involve deeper engagement and improve over the existing ASEAN FTAs with Dialogue Partners. It was meant to account for the differing levels of development among participating members. These brought many challenges, particularly because RCEP negotiation was the first of its kind and had no precedence to emulate. The negotiation involved three sets of dynamics among the participating members—between ASEAN members, between ASEAN and FTA partners, and among the six FTA partners. While the ASEAN members and ASEAN and FTA partners have worked together on economic integration for a while, the negotiation among the FTA partners proved difficult as few had trade agreements with one another. In addition, RCEP negotiating members are at different stages of development and have different market structures.[6] This meant that some negotiating members were more interested than others in reaching agreement. Although the flexibility clause built into the RCEP framework was expected to help break any deadlock and protect disparate national interests, critics also felt that it would limit change or curtail greater liberalization (Basu Das 2015a).

Given the difficulties, RCEP negotiations took 8 years to reach completion. Despite being an original negotiating member, India decided to opt out of the Agreement in November 2019.

The RCEP is often termed as megaregional. As of 2020, its member countries together accounted for about 31% ($26.1 trillion) of global GDP and 29.7% (2.3 billion) of the total population. The countries together accounted for about 29% of global merchandise trade ($10 trillion), which had earlier grown from 20% in 2000 to 25.5% in 2010, showing its further potential under RCEP's trade liberalization and facilitation measures and its commitments on regulatory coherence. When implemented, it is estimated that RCEP will increase members' income by 0.6%, adding $245 billion to regional income by 2030. It is also expected to add 2.8 million jobs to regional employment (Park, Petri, and Plummer 2021).

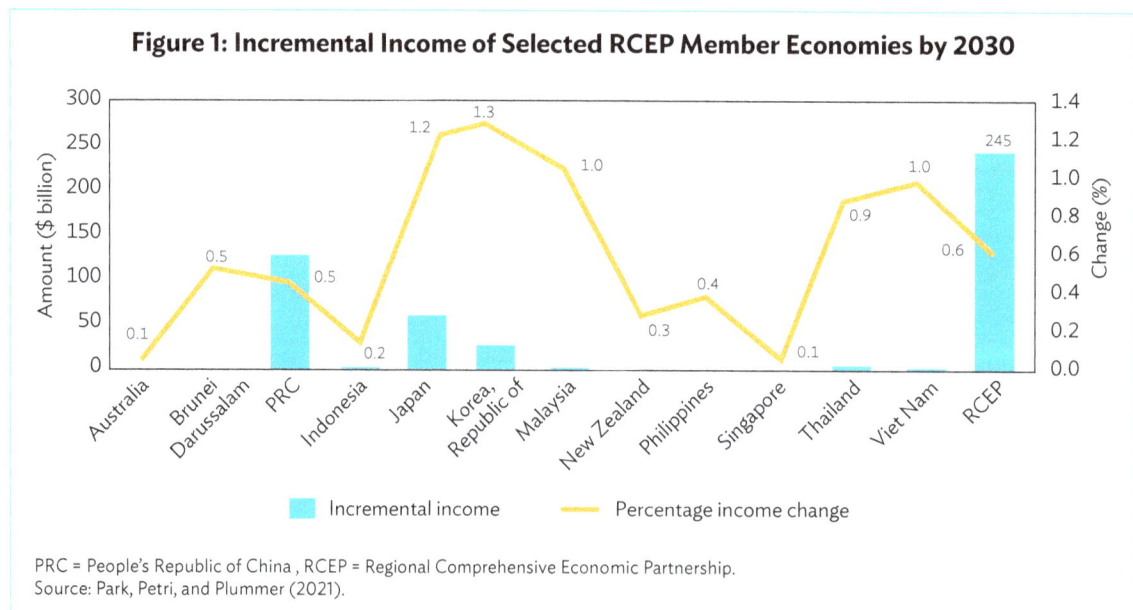

Figure 1: Incremental Income of Selected RCEP Member Economies by 2030

PRC = People's Republic of China , RCEP = Regional Comprehensive Economic Partnership.
Source: Park, Petri, and Plummer (2021).

---

[6] The RCEP members' development varies not only in terms of income but also in terms of human resource, infrastructure, regulations, and governance. Most ASEAN member countries and the Republic of Korea are more open economies with growth dependent on exports and foreign direct investment; while other countries, such as the PRC, and Indonesia, have large domestic markets to fuel their economy.

The legal text of RCEP consists of 20 chapters, ranging from trade and investment liberalization to removing regulatory barriers in services and improving business conditions through regulatory coherence in issues such as government procurement, e-commerce, intellectual property protection, competition policy. The agreement has open accession architecture, as new members can join 18 months after the agreement becomes effective. While Hong Kong, China has already shown interest in joining the pact, India, as an original RCEP negotiating member, enjoys a fast-track procedure of accession as it gets a waiver from the 18 months' timeframe requirement (Article 20.9).

The RCEP differs in membership, scope, and depth when compared to the Comprehensive and Progressive Agreement for Trans-Pacific Partnership (CPTPP), another relatively new megaregional agreement. Figure 2 and Table 2 show the differentiating factors across these agreements. On membership, it is noteworthy that four of the ASEAN members (Brunei Darussalam, Malaysia, Singapore, and Viet Nam) have membership in both RCEP and CPTPP, while six countries (Cambodia, Indonesia, the Lao PDR, Myanmar, the Philippines, and Thailand) are members of RCEP but not CPTPP. For non-ASEAN members, five countries are divided into two groups: three of them (Australia, Japan, and New Zealand) are members of both RCEP and CPTPP while two (the PRC and the Republic of Korea) have only joined RCEP. CPTPP became effective on 30 December 2018 after seven countries ratified the Agreement. The scope of CPTPP is larger as its provisions cover state-owned enterprises, labor and environment, business facilitation, and others, and it is often said to be deeper than the RCEP.

A big challenge for RCEP is to live up to the expectation of being an effective newcomer in the Asia trade scene, bringing impetus to trade liberalization and many other issues evolving in Asia and the Pacific. As discussed in this report, RCEP appears to follow the "ASEAN way" of managing regional trade integration through a combined agenda of implementation and built-in provisions to achieve greater trade liberalization, rather than through firm commitments at the outset and as contained in the original text, as is the case with the CPTPP. Simply put, RCEP needs to prove its value-added to firms and investors relative to the existing network of FTAs that will continue to be in place and may further develop. While it is difficult to assess how effectively firms have used Asian FTA networks, RCEP trade and investment liberalization will be assessed against other major agreements.

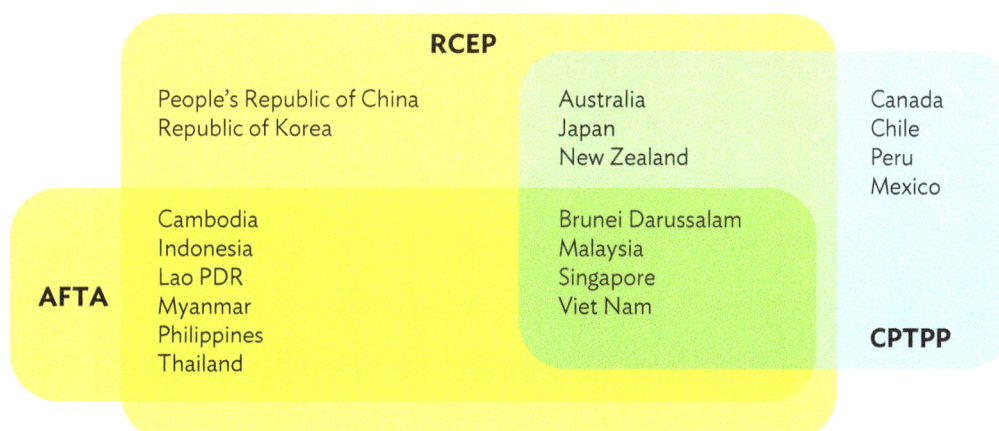

Figure 2: RCEP Members and Selected Regional Trade Agreements

RCEP

People's Republic of China
Republic of Korea

Australia
Japan
New Zealand

Canada
Chile
Peru
Mexico

AFTA

Cambodia
Indonesia
Lao PDR
Myanmar
Philippines
Thailand

Brunei Darussalam
Malaysia
Singapore
Viet Nam

CPTPP

AFTA = ASEAN Free Trade Agreement, CPTPP = Comprehensive and Progressive Agreement for Trans-Pacific Partnership, Lao PDR = Lao People's Democratic Republic, RCEP = Regional Comprehensive Economic Partnership.
Source: Asian Development Bank.

Table 2: Chapters in RCEP and CPTPP

Categories	RCEP Chapters	CPTPP Chapters
Trade in Goods	Trade in Goods	National Treatment and Market Access for Goods
	Rules of Origin	Rules of Origin and Origin Procedures
		Textile and Apparel Goods
	Customs Procedures and Trade Facilitation	Customs Administration and Trade Facilitation
	Sanitary and Phytosanitary Measures	Sanitary and Phytosanitary Measures
	Standards, Technical Regulations, and Conformity Assessment Procedures	
	Trade Remedies	Trade Remedies
		Technical Barriers to Trade
Trade in Services	Trade in Services	Cross-Border Trade in Services
		Financial Services
		Telecommunications
Movement of Persons	Temporary Movement of Natural Persons	Temporary Entry for Business Persons
Investment	Investment	Investment
Business Environment	Intellectual Property	Intellectual Property
	Electronic Commerce	Electronic Commerce
	Competition	Competition Policy
	Small and Medium Enterprises	Small and Medium-Sized Enterprises
	Economic and Technical Cooperation	Cooperation and Capacity Building
	Government Procurement	Government Procurement
		State-Owned Enterprises and Designated Monopolies
		Labor
		Environment
		Competitiveness and Business Facilitation
		Development
		Regulatory Coherence
		Transparency and Anti-Corruption
General Provisions and Dispute Settlement	General Provisions and Exceptions	Exceptions and General Provisions
	Institutional Provisions	Administrative and Institutional Provisions
	Dispute Settlement	Dispute Settlement
	Final Provisions	Final Provisions

CPTPP = Comprehensive and Progressive Agreement for Trans-Pacific Partnership, RCEP = Regional Comprehensive Economic Partnership.
Source: Compiled by the authors based on RCEP and CPTPP legal texts.

This report is divided into six parts and 19 chapters, covering all the key provisions of the RCEP trade agreement. Each chapter outlines the scope and objective and provides a preliminary assessment of the legal text. The chapters also compare RCEP commitments to those of CPTPP, WTO, and ASEAN Trade in Goods Agreement (ATIGA), as necessary. This report concludes with discussion on the way forward.

Part II
Trade in Goods

2. Trade in Goods

The Determinants of Effective Market Access

Market access on trade in goods is the most traditional form of trade liberalization. It still covers a significant part of modern trade agreements and countries continue to consider tariffs as the most effective form of protection in the context of an FTA.

Before examining the content of Chapter 2 – Trade in Goods in the RCEP Agreement, and its possible effects on trade liberalization, it is important to focus on the main determinants of "effective" market access. Potential benefits to RCEP countries come from the additional market access compared to the countries' participation in existing FTAs. As Figure 3 shows, RCEP's additional coverage of members' exports applies only to three countries: the PRC, Japan, and the Republic of Korea, with Japan being, by far, the main beneficiary.

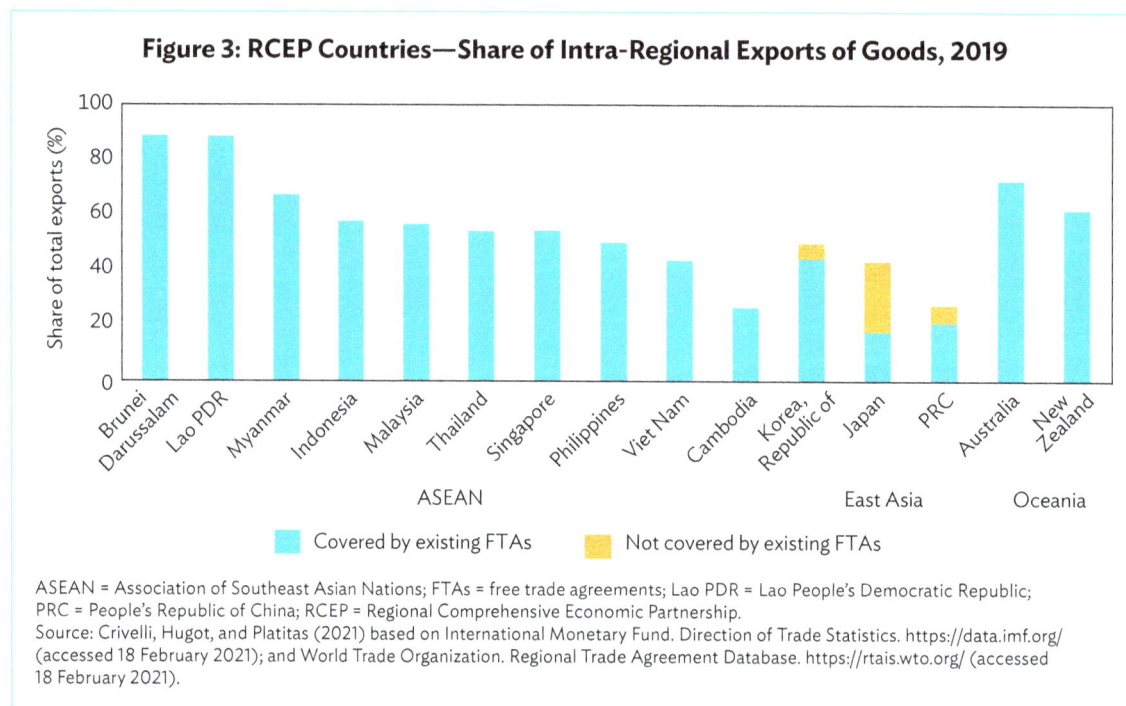

Figure 3: RCEP Countries—Share of Intra-Regional Exports of Goods, 2019

ASEAN = Association of Southeast Asian Nations; FTAs = free trade agreements; Lao PDR = Lao People's Democratic Republic; PRC = People's Republic of China; RCEP = Regional Comprehensive Economic Partnership.
Source: Crivelli, Hugot, and Platitas (2021) based on International Monetary Fund. Direction of Trade Statistics. https://data.imf.org/ (accessed 18 February 2021); and World Trade Organization. Regional Trade Agreement Database. https://rtais.wto.org/ (accessed 18 February 2021).

As an example, since there was no preexisting FTA between the PRC and Japan, the share of Japanese products subject to tariffs in the PRC has been estimated to fall from 86% to 8%. However, these estimates are subject to several assumptions: (i) full coverage of products subject to tariff phaseout under RCEP; (ii) full implementation by the end of the transition period; and (iii) full utilization of trade preferences (i.e., full compliance with ROO), as discussed on page 10 of this report.

In reality, tariff dismantling extends over 20 years for some RCEP partners and the full utilization of trade preferences under the Agreement is conditional upon compliance with ROO. Thus, after netting back these caveats the picture may be quite different.

The potential attraction for firms using RCEP is high given the important preference margins—the difference between the MFN applied rate of duty and the preferential rate. As shown in Figure 4, MFN tariff rates (simple average across products) on intraregional imports vary from 0.3% in Brunei Darussalam to 13.1% in the Republic of Korea with an average of 5.6% for all RCEP countries. Only four RCEP members (Australia, Brunei Darussalam, New Zealand, and Singapore) have MFN tariff rates below the RCEP average. This leaves ample scope for significant preference margins in the majority of RCEP economies.

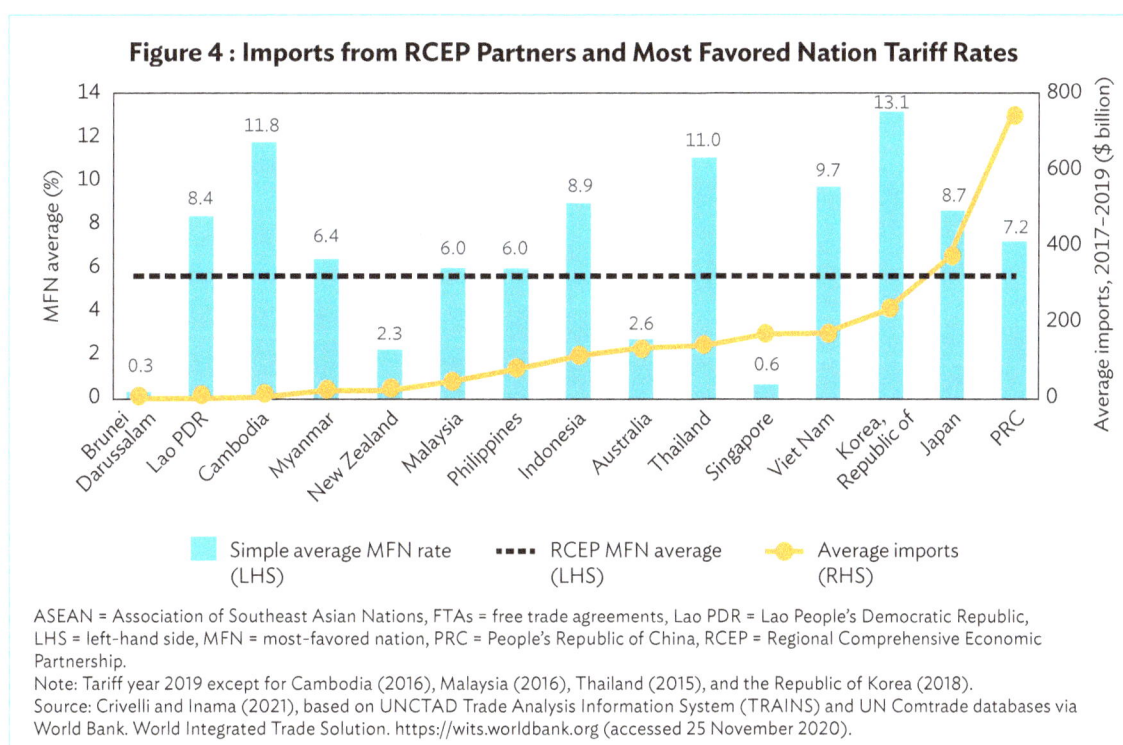

Figure 4 : Imports from RCEP Partners and Most Favored Nation Tariff Rates

ASEAN = Association of Southeast Asian Nations, FTAs = free trade agreements, Lao PDR = Lao People's Democratic Republic, LHS = left-hand side, MFN = most-favored nation, PRC = People's Republic of China, RCEP = Regional Comprehensive Economic Partnership.
Note: Tariff year 2019 except for Cambodia (2016), Malaysia (2016), Thailand (2015), and the Republic of Korea (2018).
Source: Crivelli and Inama (2021), based on UNCTAD Trade Analysis Information System (TRAINS) and UN Comtrade databases via World Bank. World Integrated Trade Solution. https://wits.worldbank.org (accessed 25 November 2020).

Measuring the Benefits of Trade Liberalization

Measuring the benefits of trade liberalization is not an easy exercise. Banga, Gallagher, and Sharma (2021) assess the trade impact of RCEP using a partial equilibrium model. The results of the simulations show that tariff liberalization under RCEP will cause the existing balance of trade of ASEAN to deteriorate relative to other RCEP countries by 6% a year, while the balance will improve for some of the non-ASEAN countries in RCEP.

According to this study, the maximum balance of trade gains will go to Japan, followed by New Zealand. Post-RCEP, trade balances will worsen for most ASEAN countries. The results show that imports from the PRC increase for ASEAN countries, except for the Lao PDR and Viet Nam. However, Japan and the Republic of Korea are the main sources of increases in PRC's imports. These results need to be interpreted with caution. First, trade effects under such partial equilibrium model are based on static assumptions where the trade effects and balance of payments results widely depend on ex ante trade flows. This may tilt the overall effects toward those countries that participate more in international trade, like the PRC, Japan, and the Republic of Korea, while showing losses for those countries that are ex ante accounting for lower trade volumes. Second, the model does not take in account intersectoral effects like foreign direct investment (FDI) moving toward least developed countries or other RCEP partners to benefit from the competitive environment generated by trade liberalization together with lower labor costs and other investment incentives. Third, in most studies using partial or general equilibrium models, full utilization of trade preferences and full implementation of the Agreement by the end of the transitional phase is assumed. Fourth, in the context of global value chains, inputs are crossing borders several times, magnifying the costs of protection. Therefore, the benefits from a reduction or elimination of tariff and nontariff barriers, coordinated among FTA member countries, become much larger for global value chains than for conventional trade.

The potential gains of value-chain linkages are especially significant in the RCEP region (Figure 5). According to UNCTAD (2020), intraregional value chain trade has grown very fast in recent years, reaching $1.5 trillion in 2017. While today the PRC, Japan, the Republic of Korea, and a few ASEAN countries are key hubs, the smaller economies are expected to increasingly integrate into intraregional value chains as a consequence of RCEP implementation.

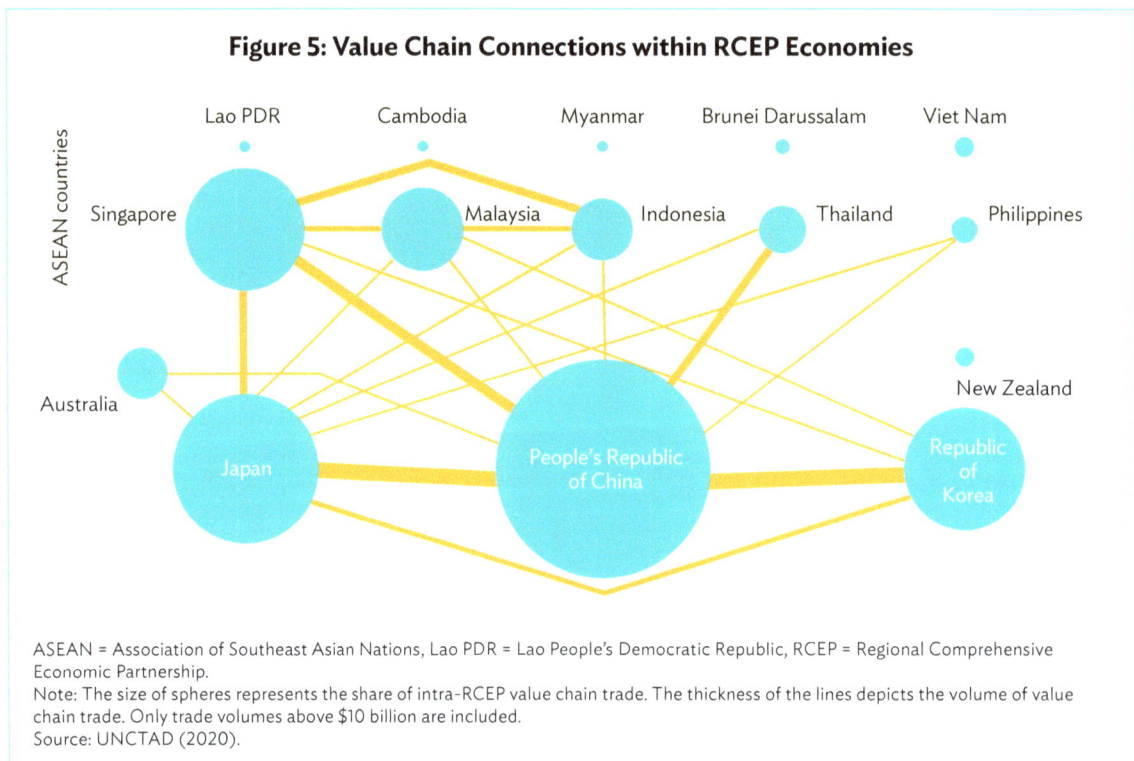

Figure 5: Value Chain Connections within RCEP Economies

ASEAN = Association of Southeast Asian Nations, Lao PDR = Lao People's Democratic Republic, RCEP = Regional Comprehensive Economic Partnership.
Note: The size of spheres represents the share of intra-RCEP value chain trade. The thickness of the lines depicts the volume of value chain trade. Only trade volumes above $10 billion are included.
Source: UNCTAD (2020).

Trade Liberalization in Practice

In order to better appreciate the trade effects of RCEP, Inama and Crivelli (2021 and 2022) consider the example of a laser manufactured in the Republic of Korea from parts originating in Japan (Figure 6). With no RCEP agreement in place, Japanese parts needed to manufacture the laser are subject to an MFN duty of 8% when imported into the Republic of Korea.[7] A duty of 2.4% is applied when the finished laser is exported to the PRC, assuming that the rules of origin (ROO) under the PRC-Korea FTA are met.[8] If ROO requirement is not met, an MFN tariff of 6% will be paid.[9] In contrast, with full implementation of RCEP commitments, no duties will be collected when ROO and related procedures are complied with. Most importantly, given RCEP diagonal cumulation (further discussed in Chapter 3), inputs from Japan will be considered as originating in RCEP, making it easier for Korean manufacturers to comply with the rule of origin when exporting the final good to the PRC.

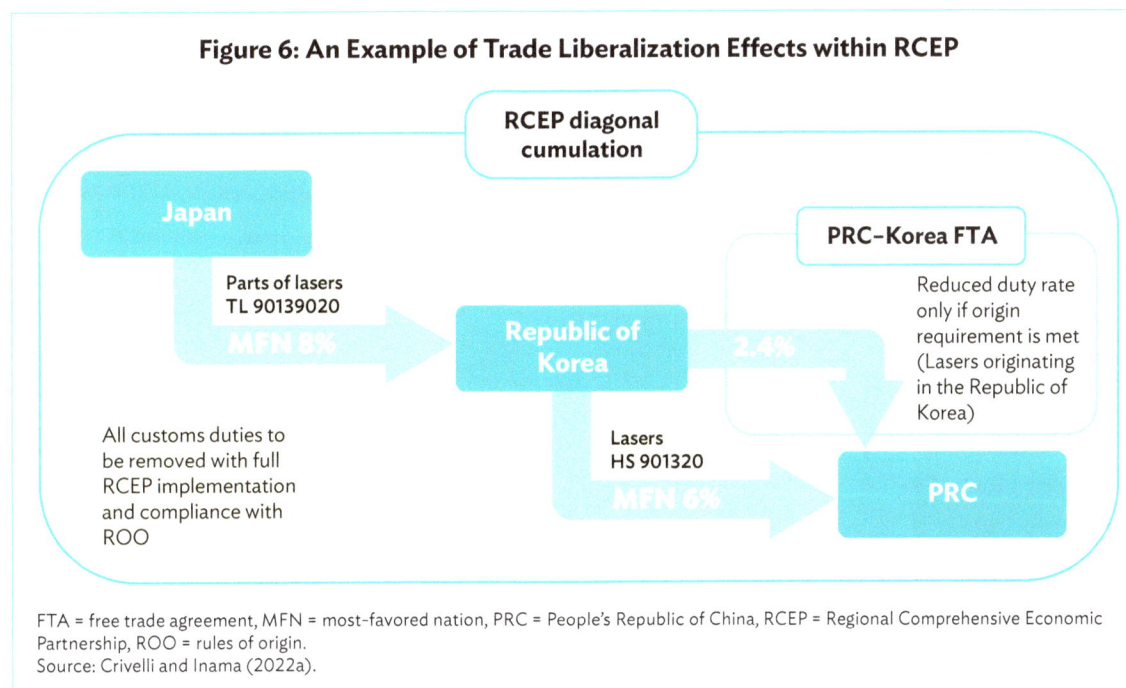

Figure 6: An Example of Trade Liberalization Effects within RCEP

FTA = free trade agreement, MFN = most-favored nation, PRC = People's Republic of China, RCEP = Regional Comprehensive Economic Partnership, ROO = rules of origin.
Source: Crivelli and Inama (2022a).

It follows that the conspicuous savings generated by trade liberalization can only be captured if ROO and associated procedures are adhered to. Studies assessing the value of RCEP should therefore account for all the variables and determinants of market access that are not only tariffs but also ROO and utilization rates.[10]

However, as Hayakawa, Urata, and Yoshimi (2020) point out, the emergence of megaregional trade agreements, like RCEP in a region with a preexisting network of FTAs, is likely to further complicate the trading environment as the "noodle bowl" of overlapping trade agreements gains significance. It is argued that when multiple preferential tariff schemes are available, exporters' choice of a given scheme depends on the coverage of products, the extent of tariff reduction, and the ease of complying with ROO. These dimensions should all be accounted for when designing megaregional trade agreements to encourage their utilization.

---

[7]   Parts of lasers classified under the Korean tariff line (TL) 90139020.

[8]   Laser of subheading 901320 of Harmonized Commodity Description and Coding System (HS).

[9]   Preferential tariff of 2020 extracted from Ministry of Commerce. http://ftatax.mofcom.gov.cn/(accessed in October 2021).

[10] This utilization rate is the ratio of the value of imports that benefited from preferences with the value of dutiable imports eligible for the preferential treatment. Dutiable imports exclude duty-free trade that can by definition not benefit from any trade preference. Utilization rates are increasingly used to monitor the effective use of preferential trading arrangements of reciprocal or autonomous nature.

Hence, there is a strong case for expanding the use of utilization rates to determine which FTAs are most attractive and efficient for firms to use, and where lower utilization rates are detected, modify and reform ROO and related administrative requirements that cause such low utilization rates.

Studies have shown that utilization rates of ASEAN trade preferences are low even when they are not publicly available. This finding emerges from surveys and research as well as from official records of ASEAN meetings (JETRO 2004, Inama and Sim 2015). As has been observed in Crivelli, Inama, and Kasteng (2021), low utilization rates are mostly linked to inadequate ROO and related administrative procedures.

The RCEP members should therefore consider utilization rates and an accompanying rigorous analysis as a valid monitoring and evaluation tool for undertaking early diagnoses of conditions where RCEP is underutilized and resolve the potential pockets of low utilization through the Agreement's built-in consultative and intergovernmental mechanisms.

Main Provisions in RCEP and CPTPP

Chapter 2 on market access on trade in goods provides enhanced transparency on import licensing procedures, commitments to pave the way for tariff transpositions of the different versions of the Harmonized Commodity Description and Coding System (HS),[11] and a forum for cooperation on good regulatory practice in measures affecting trade in goods.

As for ATIGA, the chapter also provides a mechanism to address nontariff barriers maintained by an RCEP country by establishing a consultation mechanism. Such consultation does not seem to have been used effectively under ATIGA and it remains to be seen if better use will be made under RCEP (EABC 2019).

Inspired again by ATIGA, RCEP contains a work program on sectoral initiatives, which provides an opportunity to seek further sector-specific obligations aimed at reducing unnecessary barriers to trade in specific sectors. RCEP parties have also reaffirmed their commitment to eliminate agricultural export subsidies and to work together to prevent their reintroduction in any form.

In some current FTAs, provisions regulate the relations with previous or future FTAs with third Parties, either making sure that previous tariff liberalization is not extended to other Parties or governing how further tariff liberalization efforts with a third party are or are not automatically extended to the other Parties. This is not the case in RCEP, where the relations of RCEP with other previous and future FTAs are not regulated.

One systemic and important difference between RCEP and CPTPP is the structure and architecture of tariff offers. As outlined in Table 2, CPTPP partners have opted for one single tariff offer vis-à-vis all other partners. In contrast, many RCEP countries have opted for differentiated tariff schedules: different schedules and phaseout of customs duties depending on the RCEP partner.

---

[11]   Tariff commitments on the Harmonized Commodity Description and Coding System (HS) that is subject to modifications and updating at regular intervals (roughly every 5 years) to ensure that it reflects changes in technology and patterns of international trade. Each HS revision changes the tariff commitments while ROO based on the change of tariff classification in FTAs need to be transposed into the revised nomenclature. Experiences show that this transposition process has been used to undermine tariff commitments. RCEP contains rules that should ensure future transpositions are carefully managed and verified.

As pointed out by Elms (2021), at end of the negotiating process, officials wrote 38 different tariff schedules with very long timelines, of 20 years or even slightly more. Some countries (such as Australia, Brunei Darussalam, Cambodia, the Lao PDR, Malaysia, New Zealand, Singapore, and Thailand) created a single tariff schedule to apply equally to all other trading partners. Japan used what might be termed a "hybrid" schedule. It has only one document and most of the tariff lines are applicable to all RCEP countries. However, some specific lines include different tariff rates and reduction timelines for different Parties. The PRC, Indonesia, the Republic of Korea, the Philippines, and Viet Nam opted instead for separate schedules to cover tariffs, as shown in Table 3, which compares the RCEP and CPTPP FTAs differentiated offers of tariff reduction schedules of each member country.

Table 3: Differentiated Offers for Tariff Schedules

Countries	RCEP	CPTPP	
	Partners receiving differentiated offers	Partners receiving differentiated offers	Partners receiving other forms of differentiated treatment
RCEP and CPTPP members			
Australia	–	–	Japan
Brunei Darussalam	–	–	–
Japan	ASEAN, Australia, PRC, Republic of Korea, New Zealand	–	Australia, Canada, Chile, New Zealand
Malaysia	–	–	–
New Zealand	–	–	Japan
Singapore	–	–	–
Viet Nam	ASEAN, Australia, PRC, Japan, New Zealand, Republic of Korea	–	–
RCEP or CPTPP members			
Cambodia	–	N/A	N/A
PRC	ASEAN, Australia Japan, New Zealand, Republic of Korea	N/A	N/A
Indonesia	ASEAN, Australia, PRC, Japan, New Zealand, Republic of Korea	N/A	N/A
Lao PDR	–	N/A	N/A
Myanmar	–	N/A	N/A
Philippines	Australia, PRC, Japan, New Zealand, Republic of Korea	N/A	N/A
Korea, Republic of	ASEAN, Australia, PRC, Japan, New Zealand	N/A	N/A
Thailand	–	N/A	N/A
Canada	N/A	–	Japan
Chile	N/A	–	Australia, Canada, Japan, Malaysia, Mexico, Peru, Viet Nam
Mexico	N/A	–	Australia, Brunei Darussalam, Canada, Japan, Malaysia, New Zealand, Singapore, Viet Nam
Peru	N/A	–	–

ASEAN = Association of Southeast Asian Nations, CPTPP = Comprehensive and Progressive Agreement for Trans-Pacific Partnership, Lao PDR = Lao People's Democratic Republic, N/A = not available, PRC = People's Republic of China, RCEP = Regional Comprehensive Economic Partnership.
Note: The last column refers to a scenario where a member country has differentiated treatment regarding specific goods for a certain country, but not a differentiated offer for tariff reductions for all goods comprehensively. – means no differential offer.
Source: Compiled by the authors based on RCEP and CPTPP legal texts.

The result of these differentiated offers is that the tariff rate and phaseout period may vary for the same product identified at a national tariff line level. This creates an additional layer of complexity to use RCEP tariff preferences extending to ROO and related administrative requirements.

Differentiated Offers and "Tariff Differentials"

As outlined in the previous section, the corollary of adopting differentiated tariff offers in RCEP entails that tariff phaseouts may vary between partners. It follows that a provision should be included to regulate this situation and determine the country of final origin when different countries have been involved in the production of a good and different preferential tariffs apply.

Article 2.6 in RCEP,[12] titled "Tariff differentials", is probably the most important article in Chapter 2 since it regulates in seven paragraphs the criteria that have to be progressively adopted to administer such differentials. These paragraphs apply a sequenced approach for determining how to apply tariff differentials and make references to the criteria adopted in the specific tariff schedules of RCEP countries. It follows that not only are there differentiated offers but also different criteria that apply tariff differentials depending on the specific tariff schedules.

For instance, the PRC's tariff schedule contains the following provision:

"For the purposes of this Appendix: (a) additional requirement means the requirement that an exporting Party of an originating good is the Party where no less than 20 per cent of the total value of the originating good has been added in the production of that originating good, as calculated, mutatis mutandis, under Article 3.5 (Calculation of Regional Value Content).[13]"

As can be imagined, administering such a tariff differential provision may become quite a complex exercise during RCEP implementation and daunting for administrators and firms alike.

A similar but much simpler and pragmatic provision is contained in CPTPP, which provides that the importing party:

"[S]hall apply the rate of customs duty for the originating good of the Party where the last production process, other than a minimal operation, occurred. 9. For the purposes of paragraph 8, a minimal operation is: (a) an operation to ensure the preservation of a good in good condition for the purposes of transport and storage; (b) packaging, re-packaging, breaking up of consignments or putting up a good for retail sale, including placing a good in bottles, cans, flasks, bags, cases or boxes; and (c) mere dilution with water or another substance that does not materially alter the characteristics of the good.[14]"

In simple words, CPTPP adopts a single criterion for determining the country of origin for the application of tariff differentials: the country where the last production process has taken place, unless such process is a minimal operation. This pragmatic approach also comes from CPTPP not having used general differentiated schedules to the same extent as RCEP, since there was less chance of tariff circumvention.

---

[12]   Article 2.6 "Tariff Differentials" in RCEP Chapter 2: Trade in Goods.

[13]   Paragraph 1 of the "China Appendix" in relation to paragraph 3 of Article 2.6 ("Tariff Differentials").

[14]   Chapter 2, Section (b) of Annex 2D titled "Tariff Commitments".

Another important feature is the notable fact that certain ASEAN countries have included a separate tariff schedule that applies to other ASEAN partners under RCEP. In other words, even as ASEAN countries have negotiated as a bloc, they have chosen not to transpose into RCEP the tariff liberalization achieved under ATIGA. This, in turn, means that RCEP is an entirely new FTA for ASEAN countries that wish to trade with each other using RCEP. A country offers a buffet of trade agreements for the private sector to choose from. In a nutshell, if a firm wishes to use the favorable cumulation provisions under RCEP, duties may be applicable even as the previous FTAs had abolished them. While this gives the impression of a backtracking from previous commitments under ATIGA, this situation may be explained by rules of origin and cumulation benefits that are instrumental in the negotiation and implementation of trade agreements as they can potentially compensate for reduced preference margin.

Overall, the analysis of tariff commitments under RCEP[15] shows (i) 35% of the tariff lines are already duty-free and so RCEP has no potential for trade liberalization; (ii) potential for trade liberalization exists; and (iii) the tariff-phasing down is long, complex, and incomplete (see this report's Appendix 1 on tariff schedules), with customs duties still applied to 11% of intraregional trade after 20 years. However, as usual the devil is in the details since only an accurate analysis of tariff and product-specific rules of origin (PSROs) and a cross-check among FTAs may show a firm the best FTA and ROO pair it needs to use to get the most favorable treatment.

---

[15] See Crivelli and Inama (2022a) and Crivelli, Inama, and Pearson (2022) for further details on the tariff structure of RCEP and ROO.

3. Rules of Origin

Rules of Origin and Related Administrative Procedures

The RCEP's rules of origin (ROO) have been greeted as "unified ROO across much of the region to replace a mishmash of bilateral trade deals" (*Financial Times* 2020). As pointed out by Crivelli and Inama (2021, 2022a), the potential of RCEP of acting as unifying factor and common ROO denominator derives from the fact that under RCEP's ROO it is possible to consider inputs originating from other RCEP partners as local content to comply with ROO requirements. This possibility is defined as "cumulation" and features under different modalities and geographical coverage in each FTA.

In simple words, cumulation means that to meet the regional value content (RVC) ad valorem percentage, mostly set at 40% of free on board price, an RCEP firm can count the value of other inputs originating from other RCEP countries as domestic inputs to meet the 40% requirement.

Given the participation in RCEP of the PRC, Japan, and the Republic of Korea, among the biggest and most competitive providers of inputs and intermediate products in the world, it is clear that compliance is greatly facilitated thanks to cumulation possibilities of RCEP given its wide geographical coverage.

However, as discussed in the preceding section, an RCEP firm using cumulation has to be aware of the application of the tariff preference and the related rules of application to be sure that the expected preferential margin is applied by the importing RCEP partner that has adopted a tariff differentiation schedule.

The examination of the text on cumulation contained in Article 3.4 of RCEP clearly indicates that the RCEP Parties have yet to reach a clear view on the scope and nature of the cumulation since they provide for 5 years to develop a suitable regulation mechanism. In contrast, the CPTPP text in Article 3.10 allows ample scope for cumulation since both kinds of cumulation of originating materials (diagonal cumulation) and full cumulation (cumulation of working and processing) are provided for.

Both Chapter 3 – Rules of Origin in the RCEP Agreement and CPTPP texts have deliberately chosen not to address a crucial issue related to cumulation in the context of the ROO protocol, but do so in the respective Chapter 2 on national treatment and market access for goods.

However, RCEP's ROO and related administrative requirements remain complex and may become a formidable obstacle to utilization of cumulation and RCEP potentialities. In principle, RCEP allows any exporter to self-certify product origin. However, this provision comes into force only in 10–20 years, depending on the schedule of a country, and it can be delayed by notifying other member countries. Meantime, certificates of origin can be issued only by government bodies or approved exporters, leaving scope for diverging practices by national customs administrations.

The RCEP's ROO are product-specific, as they are in most current FTAs. An initial calculation shows there are around 2,076 product-specific rules of origin (PSROs) in RCEP, which compares with 2,735 in ATIGA and 2,959 in CPTPP.

Detailed Analysis of RCEP's Rules of Origin

The ROO chapter follows the usual setting and patterns for determining ROO and related administrative procedures. It has two sections:

(i) **Section A: ROO.** This contains articles on defining originating goods, divided between goods wholly obtained or produced, and goods where more than one country has taken part in the production process. For this latter category of goods, the Annex 3A on Product-Specific Rules sets out requirements for determining originating status. Other elements covered under this section are the treatment applied to packing and packaging materials and containers for transportation and shipment, and the treatment of accessories, spare parts, and tools.

(ii) **Section B: Operational Certification Procedures.** This provides detailed administrative procedures for applying RCEP proof of origin, claiming preferential tariff treatment, and verifying the originating status of a good.

A potential positive development in the ROO chapter compared to ASEAN+1 FTAs is the inclusion in Section B of the declaration of origin by approved exporters. Yet its implementation is decided by national customs and much remains to be clarified in this area, as is apparent in the built-in agenda of this chapter.

Furthermore, the ROO chapter has two annexes: (i) Product-Specific Rules, which cover all tariff lines at the HS 6-digit level (Annex 3A); and (ii) Minimum Information Requirements, listing the information required for a Certificate of Origin or a Declaration of Origin (Annex 3B).

The drafting and negotiating history of RCEP ROO is long and complex and the final text reveals various compromises made during the negotiations. In June 2018 an initial draft of the main text was 111 pages long and the PSROs were contained in a different Microsoft Excel file with 6,247 lines. It reportedly took 21 meetings of the working group on RCEP ROO to write an initial draft that contained 41 articles, of which only 9 were agreed on October 2018 (21.9% of the text). This span of months alone gives an idea of the complexities of the negotiations and the time spent reaching agreement on the complete text.

The RCEP ROO are the result of the negotiating experience of ASEAN, Australia, Japan, and New Zealand. Below are some features:

(i) The cumulation provisions postpone the design of a full cumulation scheme to 5 years after the implementation of RCEP, which is a conspicuous sign of the complexities of that article.

(ii) On the issue of direct shipment, RCEP requires documentary evidence of direct shipment in a variety of forms. That is more liberal than the bill of lading requirement contained in many Asian FTAs, but is far removed from the principle of non-alteration.

(iii) RCEP contains provisions on third country invoicing and an arrangement for back-to-back certificates of origin.

(iv)   A provision in RCEP dedicated to "material used in production" is referring to intermediate materials in the United States model or absorption principle in the European Union model. This fills a conspicuous gap in previous FTAs in the region.

(v)   The text on certification and administration of ROO reflects wide divergences among RCEP parties. Some of them (e.g., the PRC, Cambodia) favor the maintenance of competent authorities and certificates of origin, while others (e.g., Australia and New Zealand) proposeexporter and/or importer declarations.

A Brief Comparison of CPTPP and RCEP and Recent Studies

Major administrations, such as in Australia, Japan, and New Zealand were involved in ROO negotiations with ASEAN countries in the context of both CPTPP and RCEP. However, CPTPP seems to be strongly inspired by the North American model, while RCEP appears to have mirrored some of the ASEAN rules of origin and their administration. A quick comparison of some key provisions (see Table 4) offers examples of approaches, some of which share similarities.

Several studies have touched upon ROO as among the key factors influencing the expected economic outcomes of CPTPP, RCEP, and other megaregional trade deals (Box 1). Importantly, future studies should focus on comparative analysis of how the CPTPP and RCEP solve the main issues affecting the drafting of ROO in Asia and the Pacific.

Box 1: Studies on Rules of Origin in RCEP and CPTPP

A 2016 study by the United States International Trade Commission, using a computable general equilibrium model, made the following observations about the impact of the original Trans-Pacific Partnership (TPP):

- Passenger Vehicles and Auto Parts: TPP ROO for passenger vehicles could have a negative impact on production of certain auto parts in the United States (US), and could facilitate US vehicle exports.

- Textiles: Initial growth in US imports from Viet Nam under TPP preferences would likely be moderated by Viet Nam's limited ability to meet the TPP's yarn-forward ROO.

- Chemicals: In addition to tariff elimination and market access, industry sources identified ROO as generally positive in helping to reduce business costs in the TPP region.

Considering the impact of the Regional Comprehensive Economic Partnership (RCEP) on the Association of Southeast Asian Nations (ASEAN), some authors question how ASEAN centrality can be reconciled with the multilateralization of regionalism. Wu (2019) recommends that to maintain the centrality of ASEAN while pursuing RCEP, the comprehensive partnership should be designed not only to facilitate the free movement of trade, services, and investments, but also to contribute to ASEAN integration. The author argues for two options: (i) create an ASEAN-origin rule like EU-origin rule, or (ii) make wide use of cumulation in the determination of the eligibility for trade preferences.

More specifically on ROO, Kniahin et al. (2019) used a quantification exercise involving 271 free trade agreement (FTAs) to show that the Comprehensive and Progressive Agreement for Trans-Pacific Partnership (CPTPP) on average is better than most US FTAs, but worse than non-reciprocal US arrangements such as the Caribbean Basin Trade Partnership Act, the African Growth and Opportunity Act , and the Generalized System of Preferences. Based on data assessments, CPTPP has both more lenient origin criteria than US FTAs and more trade-facilitating provisions, with the only exception being the US–Mexico–Canada Agreement.

A study on Viet Nam found that the country's industrial production structure is not consistent with the provisions of the CPTPP, particularly regarding the ROO. Viet Nam has to import most of its intermediate inputs due to the small scale of its domestic industries and lack of strong supporting industries. This makes it difficult for Viet Nam to meet the domestic content requirements of the CPTPP.

Sources:

D. Kniahin, D. Dinh, M. Mimouni, and X. Pichot. 2019. Global Landscape of Rules of Origin: Insights from the New Comprehensive Database. *GTAP Conference Paper*. https://www.gtap.agecon.purdue.edu/resources/download/9488.pdf.

H. H. Nguyen and Q.H. Truong. 2019. Vietnam and the CPTPP: Achievements and Challenges. *Perspective*. 41. https://www.iseas.edu.sg/images/pdf/ISEAS_Perspective_2019_41.pdf.

US International Trade Commission. 2016. *Trans-Pacific Partnership Agreement: Likely Impact on the U.S. Economy and on Specific Industry Sectors*. May. https://www.usitc.gov/publications/332/pub4607.pdf.

C. H. Wu. 2019. ASEAN at the Crossroads: Trap and Track between CPTPP and RCEP. *Journal of International Economic Law*. 23 (1). pp. 97–117.

Table 4: Rules of Origin Provisions—Comparing RCEP and CPTPP

RCEP	CPTPP
Article 3.2: Originating Goods	**Article 3.2: Originating goods**
"For the purposes of this Agreement, a good shall be treated as an originating good if it is: (a) wholly obtained or produced in a Party as provided in Article 3.3 (Goods Wholly Obtained or Produced); (b) produced in a Party exclusively from originating materials from one or more of the Parties; or (c) produced in a Party using non-originating materials, provided the good satisfies the applicable requirements set out in Annex 3A (Product-Specific Rules), and meets all other applicable requirements of this chapter.	Except as otherwise provided in this chapter, each Party shall provide that a good is originating if it is: (a) wholly obtained or produced entirely in the territory of one or more of the Parties as established in Article 3.3 (Wholly Obtained or Produced Goods); (b) produced entirely in the territory of one or more of the Parties, exclusively from originating materials; or (c) produced entirely in the territory of one or more of the Parties using non-originating materials provided the good satisfies all applicable requirements of Annex 3-D (Product-Specific Rules of Origin), and the good satisfies all other applicable requirements of this chapter.
Article 3.5 Calculation of Regional Value Content	**Article 3.5 Regional Value Content**
Methods of calculating RVC: (a) Build-Down Formula: $$RVC = \frac{FOB-VNM}{FOB} \times 100$$ (b) Build-Up method: $$RVC = \frac{VOM+DLC+DOC+Profit+OC}{FOB} \times 100$$	Methods of calculating RVC: (a) Focused Value Method: $$RVC = \frac{\text{Value of the Good}-FVNM}{\text{Value of the Good}} \times 100$$ (b) Build-Down Method: $$RVC = \frac{\text{Value of the Good}-VNM}{\text{Value of the Good}} \times 100$$ (c) Build-Up Method: $$RVC = \frac{VOM}{\text{Value of the Good}} \times 100$$ (d) Net Cost Method (for Automotive Goods Only): $$RVC = \frac{NC-VNM}{NC} \times 100$$
Article 3.6 Cumulation	**Article 3.10 Accumulation**
Goods and materials which comply with the origin requirements, and which are used in another Party as materials in the production of another good or material shall be considered to originate in the Party where working or processing of the finished good or material has taken place. The Parties will review Cumulation once all Parties or original signatories to the Agreement ratify and implement the Agreement or 5 years after the date of implementation of this Agreement, whichever comes earlier.	A good is originating if the good is produced in the territory of Party(ies) by producer(s), provided that it satisfies the origin requirements. Further, originating good or material of that is used in the production of another good in the territory of another Party(ies) is also considered as originating in the territory of the other Party. Lastly, production undertaken on a non-originating material in the territory of Party(ies) by pproducer(s) may contribute toward the originating content of a good for the purpose of determining its origin, regardless of whether that production was sufficient to confer originating status to the material itself.

continued on next page

Table 3 continued

RCEP	CPTPP
Article 3.8 Direct Consignment	**Article 3.18 Transit and Transshipment**
An originating good shall retain its originating status if the good has been transported directly from the exporting Party to the importing Party without passing through the territory of a non-Party. For goods transported through one or more Parties, other than the exporting Party and the importing Party, the good shall retain its originating status if good: (a) does not undergo any operation other than unloading, reloading, splitting up of the consignment, storing, repacking and/or labelling for the purpose of satisfying the requirements of the importing Party, or any other operation necessary to preserve it in good condition or to transport the good to the importing Party, and (b) remains under control of the customs authorities of the country or region of transit. Appropriate documentation may be requested by the Customs authorities of the Importing Party.	Originating good retains its originating status if the good has been transported to the importing Party without passing through the territory of a non-Party. If an originating good is transported through the territory of one or more non-Parties, the good retains its originating status provided that the good: (a) does not undergo any operation outside the territories of the Parties other than: unloading; reloading; separation from a bulk shipment; storing; labelling or marking required by the importing Party; or any other operation necessary to preserve it in good condition or to transport the good to the territory of the importing Party; and (b) remains under the control of the customs administration in the territory of a non-Party.
Article 15 Materials Used in Production	**Article 3.6 Materials Used in Production**
If a non-originating material is used in the production of a good, the following may be considered as originating content if: (a) The value of processing of the non-originating materials undertaken in the territory of one or more of the Parties; and (b) The value of any originating material used in the production of the non-originating material undertaken in the territory of one or more of the Parties.	Non-originating material undergoes further production will be treated as originating good and if a non-originating material is used in the production of a good, the following may be counted as originating content in calculating RVC: (a) The value of processing of the non-originating materials undertaken in the territory of one or more of the Parties; and (b) The value of any originating material used in the production of the non-originating material undertaken in the territory of one or more of the Parties.

CPTPP = Comprehensive and Progressive Agreement for Trans-Pacific Partnership, DLC = direct labor cost; DOC = direct overhead cost, FOB = free on board, FVNM = focused value of non-originating materials, NC = net cost of the good, OC = other cost, RCEP = Regional Comprehensive Economic Partnership, RVC= regional value content, VNM = value of non-originating materials, VOM=value of originating materials.
Source: Adapted from RCEP and CPTPP legal texts.

Product Specific Rules of Origin: Comparing RCEP and CPTPP

The RCEP's Agreement contains 5,205 PSROs for different HS Subheadings.

As for CPTPP, the final text provides for significantly less PSROs: 1,204 in total, of which 294 are at the HS Headings level and 910 at the HS Subheading level.

Table 5 makes a short comparison of selected PSROs of RCEP and the CPTPP.

Table 5: Product-Specific Rules of Origin—Comparison of RCEP and CPTPP

PSROs Overview			
General Description		**RCEP**	**CPTPP**
Number of PSROs		5205	1204
Level of Aggregation		HS6	HS4 (294) HS6 (910)
Proposed PSROs		Average: 3 Minimum: 2 Maximum: 4	N/A
PSRO HS Subheading Comparison			
HS Sub-heading	**Description**	**RCEP**	**CPTPP**
040610	Fresh (unripened or uncured) cheese, including whey cheese, and curd	CC or RVC40	CC
160414	Fish, whole or in pieces, but not minced: tunas, skipjack and bonito (Sarda spp.)	CC	CC
190300	Tapioca and substitutes therefore prepared from starch, in the form of flakes, grains, pearls, siftings or in similar forms.	CC	CC
200410	Potatoes	CC	CC
280300	Carbon (carbon blacks and other forms of carbon not elsewhere specified or included).	RVC40 or CTH	CTH
290110	Acyclic hydrocarbons: Saturated	RVC40 or CTH	CTSH
390110	Polymers of ethylene, in primary forms: Polyethylene having a specific gravity of less than 0.94	CTH, RVC40, or CR	RVC35 (Build-Up) or RVC45 (Build-Down) or CTH
610441	Dresses of wool or fine animal hair	CC	CC
620111	Overcoats, raincoats, car-coats, capes, cloaks and similar articles: of wool or fine animal hair	CC	CC
840120	Machinery and apparatus for isotopic separation, and parts thereof	RVC40 or CTSH	CTSH
850110	Motors of an output not exceeding 37.5	RVC40 or CTH	RVC35 (Build-Up) or RVC45 (Build-Down) or CTH
900110	Optical fibers, optical fiber bundles and cables	RVC40 or CTH	RVC35 (Build-Up) or RVC45 (Build-down) or CC

CC = change of tariff chapter; CPTPP = Comprehensive and Progressive Agreement for Trans-Pacific Partnership; CTH = change of tariff heading; CTSH = change of tariff subheading; HS = Harmonized Commodity Description and Coding System, or simply Harmonized System; PSROs = product-specific rules of origin; RCEP = Regional Comprehensive Economic Partnership; RVC = regional value content; WO = wholly obtained.
Source: Adapted from Crivelli, Inama, and Pearson (2022).

As can be seen in Figure 7, RCEP does not exclusively use a standard RVC40 rule but applies a wide range of rules, with the majority providing an alternative to exporters to comply either with a change of tariff heading or with a regional value content of 40%.[16]

Figure 7: RCEP—2,075 Individual Rules as Applied to 5,203 Subheadings

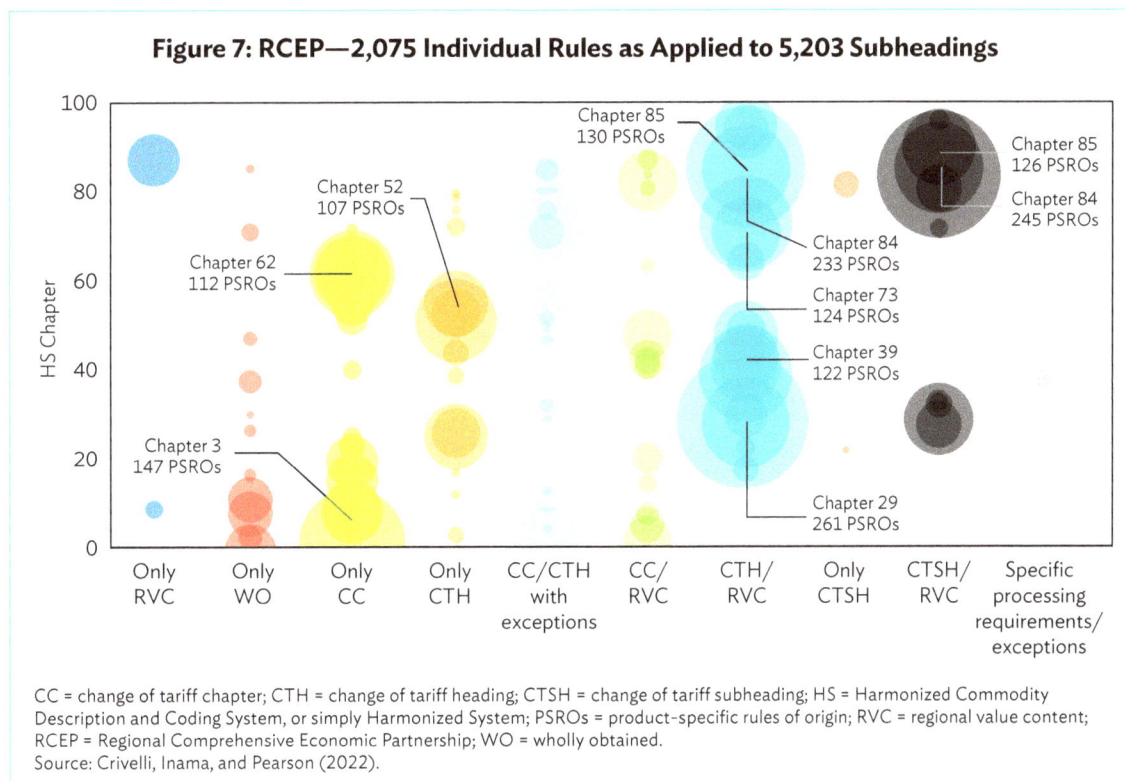

Chapter 85
130 PSROs

Chapter 85
126 PSROs

Chapter 84
245 PSROs

Chapter 52
107 PSROs

Chapter 62
112 PSROs

Chapter 84
233 PSROs

Chapter 73
124 PSROs

Chapter 39
122 PSROs

Chapter 3
147 PSROs

Chapter 29
261 PSROs

HS Chapter

x-axis categories: Only RVC | Only WO | Only CC | Only CTH | CC/CTH with exceptions | CC/ RVC | CTH/ RVC | Only CTSH | CTSH/ RVC | Specific processing requirements/ exceptions

CC = change of tariff chapter; CTH = change of tariff heading; CTSH = change of tariff subheading; HS = Harmonized Commodity Description and Coding System, or simply Harmonized System; PSROs = product-specific rules of origin; RVC = regional value content; RCEP = Regional Comprehensive Economic Partnership; WO = wholly obtained.
Source: Crivelli, Inama, and Pearson (2022).

---

[16] Detailed analysis of RCEP product-specific ROO and comparison with ATIGA and CPTPP can be found in Crivelli, Inama, and Pearson (2022).

4. Customs Procedures and Trade Facilitation

Following the substantial reduction in tariff rates in the past 25 years, customs practices and bottlenecks have become increasingly significant as a barrier or cost to trade. A study that analyzed the impact of Spain's administrative pre-shipment costs on trade volumes found that a 50% reduction in pre-shipment costs is equivalent to a 9 percentage point reduction in tariffs (Hornok and Koren 2015). Similarly, another study found a strong correlation between the volume of FDI flows to the sample countries and their ranking in the Doing Business Index of the World Bank (Corcoran and Gillanders 2015). The authors also concluded that this outcome was mostly due to the trading across the borders component of that index. Such component measures the time and cost associated with the logistics of exporting and importing goods (World Bank 2020).

Whether or not these correlations are equally strong in Asia and the Pacific, some RCEP countries need to close the gap with the world's top performers in easing trading across borders. Table 6, in fact, shows the following:

(i) Six RCEP countries rank below the world's median in the 2020 Doing Business component.

(ii) Only six countries (Australia, the PRC, Japan, the Republic of Korea, Malaysia, and Singapore) belong to the top 30% worldwide.

(iii) Performance disparities are enormous, ranging from the 36th position to 168th, out of 192 countries and territories.

(iv) Since the rankings in the Doing Business index is considered rather subjective, another indicator has been used as a comparator: the Logistics Performance Index (LPI), again developed by the World Bank, which also contains a customs component (World Bank 2018). Under the LPI, which is perhaps even more subjective, depending on surveys conducted among foreign customs operators, all RCEP countries perform much better, except for few that may catch up with their current commitments under trade facilitation.

(v) Low implementation rates of commitments under the World Trade Organization (WTO 2021) Trade Facilitation Agreement (TFA) are also observed for three RCEP economies.

(vii) In conclusion, ranking at least two scores below the global average, some RCEP countries highlighted in gray in Table 6 may require technical and/or financial assistance.

The importance of customs efficiency and, more generally, of trade facilitation has been increasingly recognized by the international community and by ASEAN as well. Trade facilitation is the only topic on which the WTO has achieved an agreement, although plurilateral, since the launch of the Doha Round in 2001, with the Bali package adopted in 2013. However, the TFA entered into force in 2017.

Trade facilitation also became common as a feature in ASEAN and ASEAN+1 agreements, though with several differences in coverage and depth of commitments. As an example, ASEAN has made significant progress in the development of an ASEAN single window, i.e., a common customs declaration document for imports, exports, and goods in transit. However, such an important trade facilitation subject as the single window does not figure in the ASEAN+1 FTAs.

Table 6: RCEP Countries—Doing Business and Logistics Performance Index Rankings, and Current Implementation Rates of TFA Commitments

	Doing Business Ranking (192 countries)	Logistics Performance Index Ranking (160 countries)	TFA—Rate of Implementation Progress (%)
Korea, Republic of	36	25	100
Australia	37	7	100
Singapore	47	6	100
Malaysia	49	43	94
China, People's Republic of	56	31	100
Japan	57	3	100
Thailand	62	36	97
New Zealand	63	13	100
Lao PDR	78	74	32
World Median	**96**	**80**	**61***
Viet Nam	104	41	27
Philippines	113	85	98
Indonesia	116	52	89
Cambodia	118	109	94
Brunei Darussalam	149	73	92

Lao PDR = Lao People's Democratic Republic, RCEP = Regional Comprehensive Economic Partnership, TFA = Trade Facilitation Agreement.
* Average rate of implementation for developing and least developed countries.
Notes: "Doing business" rates time and cost to export the product of comparative advantage and to import auto parts. The Logistics Performance Index rates the efficiency of customs and border clearance.
Sources: World Bank (2018 and 2020), World Trade Organization (2021).

The RCEP's trade facilitation chapter virtually covers the same areas as those contained in WTO's TFA and in CPTPP, such as single window, procedures for authorized operators, a risk management approach for customs control and post-clearance audits, publishing customs information, cooperation among customs authorities, and customs and trade logistics.

However, such an important trade facilitation subject as the single window is yet to be covered under the ASEAN+1 FTAs.[17]

(i) **Time limits on goods at border transit.** While TFA mentions no time limits, the two FTAs call for goods to be released within 48 hours of arrival at customs. For express consignments the time limit is reduced to 6 hours. This limit, which also applies to perishable goods in RCEP, is absent in CPTPP. This kind of "CPTPP plus" arrangement is an important advance for many RCEP countries (both developed and developing) that export perishable agricultural products, such as meat, dairy, seafood, and fresh fruit and vegetables.

(ii) **Advance rulings.** Both RCEP and CPTPP contain improved advance ruling provisions based on tariff classification, ROO, customs valuation, and a time limit of 150 days for the rulings to be issued. These provisions are especially important for trade in complex goods. Freund (2016, p. 302) explains that "For some goods, tariff classification is difficult, but an advance ruling allows importers to determine the correct classification before importation, so there are no surprises at the border. Delays on such rulings restrict trade in these complex goods."

---

[17] The hortatory language used in these provisions can nevertheless cast doubts on their credibility.

Despite the strong similarities between RCEP and CPTPP, an important area common to RCEP and TFA—though absent from CPTPP—is the special and differential treatment for developing countries. Although these countries are not mentioned as such, Chapter 4 – Customs Procedures and Trade Facilitation in the RCEP Agreement recognizes the different levels of readiness of Parties in implementing some of the commitments and allows them a longer period for their full implementation. Cambodia, the Lao PDR, Myanmar, and Viet Nam have used this special treatment to postpone implementation by 2–5 years.

After examining the contents of the two megaregional agreements, the next step is to identify what is missing from them. Freund (2016) suggests three areas for future improvements in CPTPP, which can equally be applied to RCEP:

(i)   Mandating members to use a single entry point.

(ii)   Using "hard-law" language requiring members to employ World Customs Organization standards by a given deadline.

(iii)   Introducing de minimis rules, allowing imports below a given monetary value to enter member countries duty-free. These rules would greatly benefit SMEs throughout the RCEP region (Freund 2016).

In conclusion, Chapter 4 of the RCEP Agreement contains the value added of a number of WTO-plus and CPTPP-plus clauses. However, as stressed throughout this report, value added can be realized only to the extent to which the chapter provisions are implemented, narrowing the wide gap in customs efficiency among the RCEP countries. Technical and financial assistance to the four countries already benefiting from Special and Differential Treatment can be instrumental. As pointed out at the start of this section, full implementation of the trade facilitation commitments could have a greater impact on trade liberalization and strengthening global value chains than tariff reductions alone.

5. Sanitary and Phytosanitary Measures and Technical Barriers to Trade

Trade in Asia and the Pacific is widely affected by nontariff measures (NTMs) that mostly derive from application of sanitary and phytosanitary measures (SPS) and technical barriers to trade (TBT). Repeated attempts since the establishment of AFTA have sought to reduce the incidence of NTMs with difference initiatives, including mutual recognition agreements and lately introducing a mechanism in ATIGA for the notification and elimination of nontariff measures .

However, identification of existing NTMs has been a drawn-out process in ASEAN, involving both self-reporting by member states and original inquiries by the ASEAN Secretariat. Although a mechanism is in place for the private sector to complain about alleged NTBs, the process is slow and hampered by the absence of an enforcing authority.[18]

A UNESCAP report (2019) found that over the past 2 decades applied tariffs in Asia and the Pacific have decreased in number while NTMs have proliferated. As shown in Figure 8, NTMs related to SPS and TBT show uneven but constant growth with respect to applied tariffs.

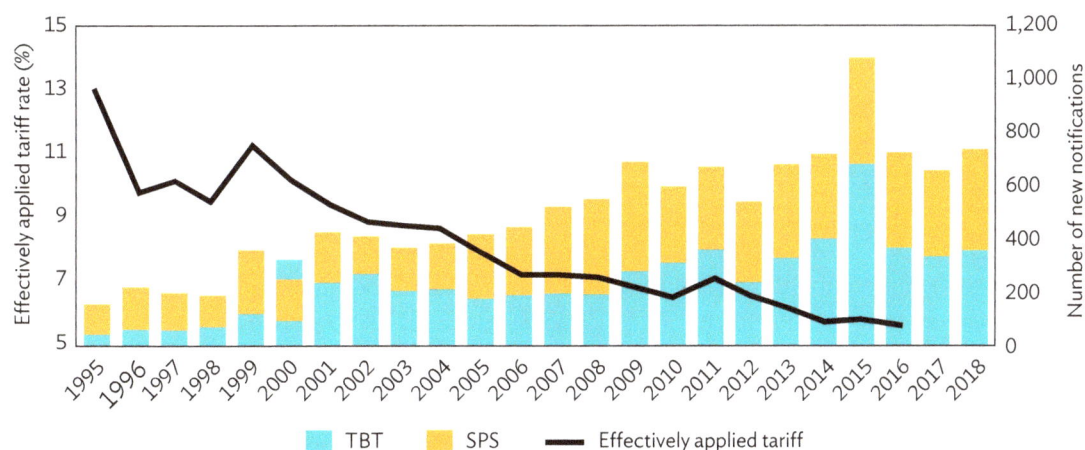

Figure 8: Average Applied Tariff and New Annual Notifications to WTO of Sanitary and Phytosanitary Measures and Technical Barriers to Trade Measures in Asia and the Pacific

SPS = sanitary and phytosanitary measures, TBT = technical barriers to trade, WTO = World Trade Organization.
Source: UNESCAP (2019).

---

18   The Economic Research Institute for ASEAN and East Asia and UNCTAD have compiled a database of ASEAN NTMs, available in the Trade Analysis Information System (TRAINS). While the database is detailed and comprehensive, elimination of NTMs remains a major issue for most economies.

In dealing with SPS and TBT, both RCEP and CPTPP uphold the basic commitments of WTO SPS and TBT Agreements, with some variations. Yet, in this vital area, the real point is to assess what can be the WTO-plus contributions of RCEP and CPTPP in leading to progressive reduction of nontariff measures.

SPS in RCEP and CPTPP

Compliance with SPS requirements is a key aspect of market access to successful and effective trade in agricultural products. In particular, this sector may provide decisive trading opportunities for countries like Australia and New Zealand and, most important, for ASEAN least developed countries neighboring the PRC and the Republic of Korea. According to the New Zealand RCEP National Interest Analysis (2020), RCEP's SPS chapter provides better outcomes than the ASEAN-Australia-New Zealand FTA (AANZFTA) in relation to the following:

(i)   Equivalence: Encouraging RCEP-importing parties to accept that goods meet their SPS requirements if the exporting RCEP demonstrates that its SPS measures achieve the same level of protection, i.e., equivalent, without having to be identical.

(ii)   Regionalization: Promoting acceptance of regional conditions, including pest-free or disease-free areas and areas of low pest or disease prevalence.

(iii) Emergency measures: If a Party adopts an emergency SPS measure that impacts on other RCEP trade, it is required to hold discussions on request and take account of information provided.

However, such an optimistic view and the abovementioned additions in relation to the AANZTA benchmark are unlikely to reduce the array and number of NTMs that were shown in Figure 8. The analysis in this section related to SPS and TBT aims at conducting a preliminary assessment based on text-based comparison of the respective provisions. The ultimate objective is to gauge whether RCEP has the tools appropriate for reducing NTMs arising from the application of SPS and TBT requirements. However, such a definitive assessment would warrant a separate study, based not only on text comparison but also on an overall review of the capacity of SPS and TBT institutions and related infrastructure.

A recent UNESCAP study compared commitments in different FTAs with a series of benchmark provisions derived from multilateral and regional commitments, mostly already included in WTO SPS and TBT Agreements and most recent FTAs (Trivedi et al. 2019). In the case of SPS, the following are the benchmarks:

(i)   Reference to the WTO Agreement on the Application of Sanitary and Phytosanitary Measures (SPS Agreement): The regional trade agreement (RTA) specifically refers to and stresses compliance with the SPS Agreement.

(ii)   Provision on information exchange and cooperation: The RTA includes a provision on exchange of information and cooperation on SPS measures.

(iii) Assigning competent authorities and contact points: The RTA specifies that all the countries should have SPS contact and/or enquiry points with whom the other countries can instantly connect to make an enquiry.

(iv)   Reference to use of international standards: The RTA encourages use of international standards for SPS measures, to conform to the relevant guidance of international standards.

(v)   Establishment of an SPS committee: The RTA partners form an SPS committee to fulfill the objectives of the SPS chapter.

(vi)   Provision on risk analysis: The RTA provides guidance on risk analysis for conformity to standards and norms and how they should be implemented and/or accepted.

(vii)   Provision on equivalence: The RTA promotes mutual recognition and acceptance of the SPS certificates issued by RTA partners, to prevent goods being tested in both the exporting and importing country.

(viii) Mutual recognition of standards: The RTA encourages mutual understanding of SPS measures taken by the RTA partners, to foster mutual confidence and demonstrate the efficiency of the programs.

(ix)   Import checks: The RTA specifies that SPS inspections should be conducted without undue delay at the border.

(x)   Provision on taking emergency measures: The RTA encourages RTA members to notify other members when they take emergency SPS measures.

(xi)   Certification of products: The RTA specifies the certification is only requested to the extent necessary to protect human, animal, or plant life or health.

(xii)   Provision on audits: The RTA includes a provision on audit specifying that the audit shall be system-based and follow the guidance of WTO SPS Committee.

(xiii) Harmonization with international standards: The RTA promotes harmonization between national and international standards, and between the parties' standards.

(xiv)   Provision on import requirement: The RTA enables acquiring relevant information about imported commodities without undue delay to ensure that available resources are managed efficiently.

(xv)   Regionalization and compartmentalization: The RTA promotes importation based on region or compartment to facilitate mutual trade.

Based on these benchmarks, a comparative analysis was carried out on 58 FTAs in the Asian region, such as ASEAN FTAs with dialogue partners and other FTAs. Trivedi et al. (2019) calculated an SPS coverage score for each of the RTAs, based on how many of the 15 benchmark provisions were contained in the selected FTAs. CPTPP ranked among the top FTAs since it included all provisions besides Harmonization with International Standards. Table 7 uses these benchmarks to compare CPTPP and RCEP.

Based on these findings, RCEP contains 11 benchmark provisions while CPTPP includes 14. It is obvious that this comparison does not investigate in detail the language used in each specific provision under examination. However, even preliminary analysis shows that while the CPTPP text does not contain substantive WTO-plus commitments, its language is relatively predictable and legally sound. RCEP seems to have softer tone and approach to its commitments..

Most important, and unlike CPTPP, RCEP does not provide for establishment of an SPS committee to take the agenda forward or a forum where experts in such a highly technical discipline as SPS can meet to make advances and help eliminate NTMs related to SPS requirements.

Table 7: A Comparison of Provisions on Sanitary and Phytosanitary Benchmarks between CPTPP and RCEP

Benchmark	CPTPP	RCEP	Comments (articles are those in RCEP)
(1) Reference to the WTO Agreement on the Application of Sanitary and Phytosanitary Measures (SPS Agreement).	X	X	Article 5.4 explicitly recalls the WTO SPS Agreement. In addition, several articles of Chapter 5 makes explicit reference to such agreement.
(2) Provision on information exchange and cooperation	X	X	Article 5.12 provides for information and exchange of information making reference to the WTO SPS Agreement.
(3) Assigning competent authorities and contact points	X	X	Article 5.15 provides for exhaustive provisions for establishing competent authorities and contact points.
(4) Reference to use of international standards	X	N/A	The reference to international standards is not present. Only Article 5.1 definition makes reference to Codex Alimentarius.
(5) Establishment of an SPS committee	X	N/A	There is no provision in Chapter 5 – Sanitary and Phytosanitary Measures of the RCEP Agreement for a dedicated committee on SPS.
(6) Provision on risk analysis	X	X	Article 5.7 deals with risk analysis making reference to WTO SPS Agreement and provides for a consultation mechanism.
(7) Provision on equivalence	X	X	Article 5.5 deals with equivalence providing for a consultation mechanism to determine and establish equivalence.
(8) Mutual recognition of standards	X	N/A	There is no express provision to develop mutual recognition.
(9) Import checks	X	X	Article 5.10 deals with import checks making reference to the WTO SPS Agreement providing for limited consultation mechanism.
(10) Provision on taking emergency measures	X	X	Article 5.11 deals with emergency measures providing for a consultation mechanism.
(11) Certification of products	X	X	Article 5.9 refers to WTO SPS Agreement and limits certification to the extent necessary to protect human, animal, or plant life or health.
(12) Provision on audits	X	X	Article 5.8 provides for audits making reference to WTO SPS committee.
(13) Harmonization with international standards	N/A	N/A	In both Agreements, there is no reference to harmonization with international standards.
(14) Provision on import requirement	X	X	Article 5.12 on transparency provides for mechanism and consultations.
(15) Regionalization, compartmentalization	X	X	Article 5.6 provides for regionalization.

N/A = not available, CPTPP = Comprehensive and Progressive Agreement for Trans-Pacific Partnership, RCEP = Regional Comprehensive Economic Partnership, SPS = sanitary and phytosanitary measures, WTO = World Trade Organization.
Source: Adapted from benchmark provisions in Trivedi et al. (2019).

Technical Barriers to Trade in RCEP and CPTPP

With regard to TBT, as in SPS, CPTPP was among the three FTAs, out of 58 considered in the study, to receive a full score of nine, i.e., CPTPP contains all the provisions that are considered key in regulating TBT.

There are nine provisions or features used to benchmark the RTAs on their TBT content:

(i) **Reference to the WTO TBT agreement.** The RTA specifically refers to and stresses compliance with the Agreement, which aims to ensure that technical regulations, standards, and conformity assessment procedures are non-discriminatory and do not create unnecessary obstacles to trade.

(ii) **Provision on dispute settlement.** The scope of the dispute settlement committee under the RTA extends to TBT-related matters.

(iii) **Provision on information exchange and cooperation.** The RTA includes a provision on exchange of information and cooperation for better implementation of the provisions.

(iv) **Reference to use of International Standards.** The RTA encourages the use of international standards to curb the cost of compliance with country-specific technical standards and norms.

(v) **Harmonization with international standards.** The RTA promotes harmonization of member's practices with international standards.

(vi) **Provision on conformity assessment procedures.** The RTA provides guidance on assessment procedures for conformity to technical standards and norms and how they should be implemented and/or accepted.

(vii) **Mutual recognition of conformity assessment procedures.** The RTA promotes mutual recognition, i.e., acceptance and recognition of the Conformity Assessment Procedures used by the RTA partners, to prevent goods being tested in both the exporting and importing country—and so save time and cost.

(viii) **Establishment of a TBT committee.** The RTA partners form a TBT committee to fulfill the objectives of the TBT chapter.

(ix) **Assigning contact points.** The RTA specifies that all the countries should have TBT contact and/or enquiry points with whom the other countries can instantly connect.

Table 8 contains a detailed comparison of the TBT provisions contained in CPTPP and RCEP.

Table 8: A Comparison of Provisions on Technical Barriers to Trade between CPTPP and RCEP

Benchmark	CPTPP	RCEP	Comments (articles in RCEP)
(1) Reference to WTO TBT agreement	X	X	Article 6.4 makes explicit reference to the WTO TBT Agreement articles and paragraphs in a similar fashion to CPTPP and provides that in case of conflict the WTO TBT Agreement will prevail.
(2) Provision on dispute settlement	X	N/A	Article 6.14 specifically provides that Chapter 19 – Dispute Settlement does not apply to Chapter 6 – Standards, Technical Regulations, and Conformity Assessment Procedures and provides for review of this clause within 3 years after entry into force.
(3) Provision on information exchange and cooperation	X	X	Article 6.9 explicitly provides for cooperation. However, such cooperation is triggered by requests from other RCEP members and does not appear to be part of a systemic effort to exchange of information and cooperation. See also paragraph 7 of Article 6.7 where information on the development of a technical regulation is provided only upon request. In the same vein, see also paragraph 4 of Article 6.6.
(4) Reference to use of international standards	X	X	Reference and recognition of international standards are made in Article 6.5 (which is clearly inspired by Article 8.5 of CPTPP) and Article 6.6 in relation to application of Article 3 of the TBT Agreement. However, it seems that articles 6.5 and 6.6 do not refer to or recommend explicitly the use of international standards. Article 6.6 is just requiring that, upon request, RCEP member states provide information in case they deviate from international standards.
(5) Harmonization with international standards	X	N/A	There is a generic reference to harmonization with international standards in paragraph 1 of Article 6.5 but there is no promotion or encouragement toward such harmonization.
(6) Provision on conformity assessment procedures	X	X	Article 6.8 deals with conformity assessment procedures making a reference to paragraph 4 of Article 5 of the WTO TBT Agreement .It also provides for mechanisms and procedures to facilitate recognition of conformity assessments procedures.
(7) Establishment of a TBT committee	X	N/A	In RCEP, there is no express provision to establish a TBT committee.
(8) Mutual recognition of conformity assessment procedures	X	N/A	There is a mention of mutual recognition as one of the options to accept conformity assessments made by other parties, but there is no strong mechanism provided to encourage and ensure mutual recognition, especially in comparison with CPTPP.
(9) Assigning contact points	X	X	Article 6.12 clearly provides for contact points to be established.

N/A = not available, CPTPP = Comprehensive and Progressive Agreement for Trans-Pacific Partnership, RCEP = Regional Comprehensive Economic Partnership, TBT = technical barriers to trade, WTO = World Trade Organization.
Source: Adapted from benchmark provisions in Trivedi et al. (2019).

As in SPS, the results of such preliminary text comparison are that the CPTPP text provides more comprehensive coverage of key benchmarks than RCEP to regulate effectively TBT in FTAs. The CPTPP includes nine provisions while RCEP includes only five.

Unlike RCEP, CPTPP includes provisions on the following topics: (i) establishment of a dedicated TBT committee, (ii) application of dispute settlement provisions, and (iii) clearer commitment and procedures for mutual recognition and harmonization with international standards.

In addition, CPTPP provides for a series of annexes that demonstrate the commitments of Parties to work further to reduce NTMs due to TBT disparities.

6. Trade Remedies

Asia was mostly the target of trade remedies for decades until the moment when Asian countries started to establish their own investigation authorities and gradually became major users of trade remedies. As outlined in Figure 9, RCEP members as a whole are among the major users of anti-dumping measures among WTO members, which is the most frequently used trade remedy.

Figure 10 shows that among RCEP members, the major users of anti-dumping measures are by far Australia and the PRC, followed by the Republic of Korea, Indonesia, Malaysia, and Thailand.

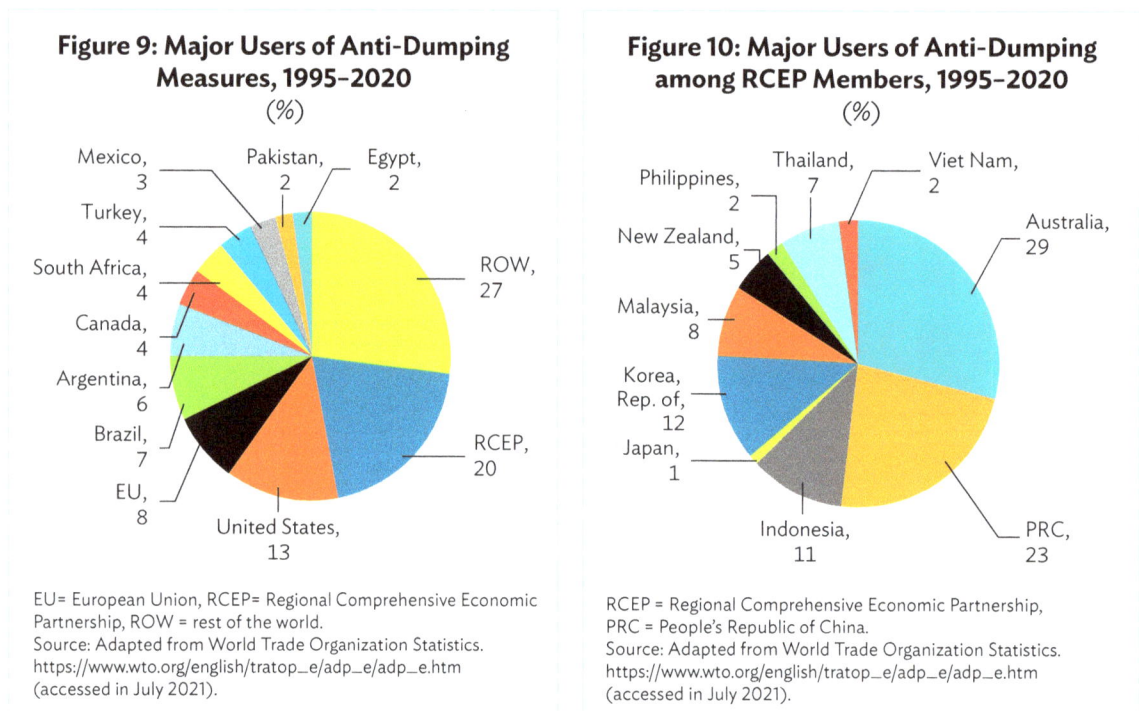

Figure 9: Major Users of Anti-Dumping Measures, 1995–2020
(%)

Mexico, 3
Pakistan, 2
Egypt, 2
Turkey, 4
South Africa, 4
Canada, 4
Argentina, 6
Brazil, 7
EU, 8
United States, 13
RCEP, 20
ROW, 27

EU= European Union, RCEP= Regional Comprehensive Economic Partnership, ROW = rest of the world.
Source: Adapted from World Trade Organization Statistics.
https://www.wto.org/english/tratop_e/adp_e/adp_e.htm (accessed in July 2021).

Figure 10: Major Users of Anti-Dumping among RCEP Members, 1995–2020
(%)

Philippines, 2
Thailand, 7
Viet Nam, 2
New Zealand, 5
Malaysia, 8
Korea, Rep. of, 12
Japan, 1
Indonesia, 11
Australia, 29
PRC, 23

RCEP = Regional Comprehensive Economic Partnership, PRC = People's Republic of China.
Source: Adapted from World Trade Organization Statistics.
https://www.wto.org/english/tratop_e/adp_e/adp_e.htm (accessed in July 2021).

The RCEP members are widely using trade remedies especially anti-dumping measures and countervailing duties against each other, as demonstrated by the recent wave of cases where the PRC has requested WTO dispute consultations with Australia regarding anti-dumping and countervailing duties (WTO 2021a). Meanwhile, Australia has requested consultations with the PRC concerning anti-dumping and countervailing duty measures imposed by the PRC on imports of bottled wine from Australia (WTO 2021b), and Japan (WTO 2021c) on anti-dumping duties imposed by the PRC on stainless steel.

Figures 11 to 13 show that the major RCEP users of anti-dumping measures are Australia, the PRC, and the Republic of Korea, and they mostly target other RCEP partners, adding another important dimension to intraregional RCEP trade.

Figure 11: Australia—Anti-Dumping Distribution

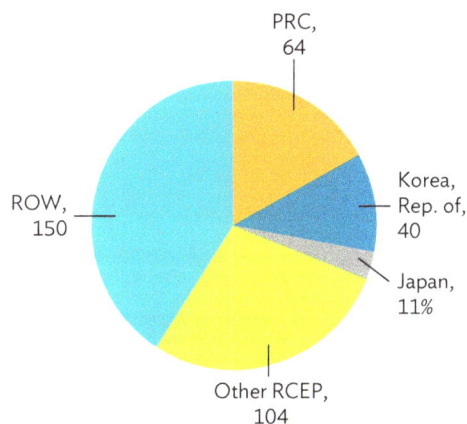

PRC, 64
Korea, Rep. of, 40
Japan, 11%
Other RCEP, 104
ROW, 150

PRC = People's Republic of China, RCEP= Regional Comprehensive Economic Partnership, ROW = rest of the world.
Source: Adapted from World Trade Organization Statistics. https://www.wto.org/english/tratop_e/adp_e/adp_e.htm (accessed in July 2021).

Figure 12: People's Republic of China— Anti-Dumping Distribution

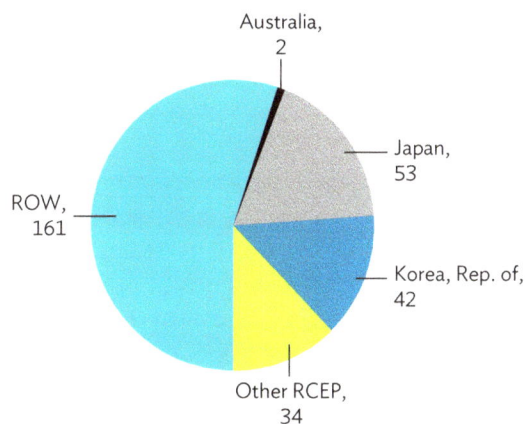

Australia, 2
Japan, 53
Korea, Rep. of, 42
Other RCEP, 34
ROW, 161

RCEP= Regional Comprehensive Economic Partnership, ROW = rest of the world.
Source: Adapted from World Trade Organization Statistics.| https://www.wto.org/english/tratop_e/adp_e/adp_e.htm (accessed in July 2021).

Figure 13: The Republic of Korea— Anti-Dumping Distribution

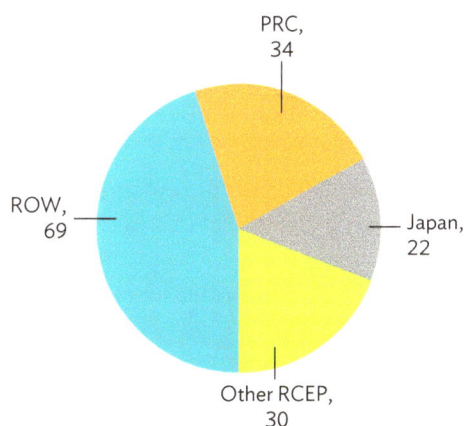

PRC, 34
Japan, 22
Other RCEP, 30
ROW, 69

PRC = People's Republic of China, RCEP= Regional Comprehensive Economic Partnership, ROW = rest of the world.
Source: Adapted from World Trade Organization Statistics. https://www.wto.org/english/tratop_e/adp_e/adp_e.htm (accessed in July 2021).

As in CPTPP and other FTAs, Chapter 7 – Trade Remedies in the RCEP Agreement makes ample reference to rights and obligations under relevant WTO agreements on trade remedies (the Agreement on Anti-Dumping, the Agreement on Subsidies and Countervailing Measures, and the Agreement on Safeguards). More specifically, the RCEP chapter draws inspiration from the CPTPP text, especially when it confirms that WTO rules apply to global safeguards (Article 7.9), and to the administration of anti-dumping and countervailing duties on trade between RCEP parties.

In a similar vein to CPTPP again, the RCEP Chapter 7 also provides procedural guarantees for on-the-spot investigation, notification, and consultation, which are usually included in FTAs. These additional features do not fundamentally alter or amplify the rights and procedures of RCEP members under the respective trade remedies provided in the WTO Agreements.

A potential WTO-plus discipline is contained in Article 7.13, titled "Prohibition of Zeroing". Zeroing is an accounting practice used by some anti-dumping investigating authorities for calculating the dumping margin to consider null the transactions showing a negative dumping margin.[19] In this way, the dumping margin is either higher, or a positive dumping margin is found where arguably no dumping has taken place. However, a closer reading of the Article 7.13 text shows a significant carve out on the prohibition of zeroing where it make reference to the rights and obligation under subparagraph 2.4.2 of Article 2 of the WTO's Agreement on Anti-Dumping. This is tantamount to leaving investigating authorities with wide discretion in applying zeroing.

The most important aspect of Chapter 7 is the importance given to safeguard measures, which takes up 9 out the chapter's 13 pages.

Under paragraph 1 of Article 7.2, the transitional RCEP safeguard measures provide for the following possibilities:

(i)   Suspend the further reduction of any rate of customs duty provided for in this Agreement on the originating good; or

(ii)   Increase the rate of customs duty on the originating good to a level not to exceed the lesser of:

(a) the most-favored-nation applied rate of customs duty in effect on the day when the transitional RCEP safeguard measure is applied; or

(b) the most-favored-nation applied rate of customs duty in effect on the day immediately preceding the date of entry into force of this Agreement for that Party.

As in any safeguard measures, the application of such measures depends on the following requirements:

(i)   a finding of a serious injury,

(ii)   a causal link of such injury in relation with imports in increased quantities, and

(iii)   subject to an investigation and a series of procedural rights.

The Parties affected by the application of transitional RCEP measures are offered compensation.

---

[19]   See the WTO glossary for adefinition: WTO. Zeroing. https://www.wto.org/english/thewto_e/glossary_e/zeroing_e.htm.

A similar provision, in similar language used in RCEP, is contained in the CPTPP text under Article 6.3, which, however, makes it clear that safeguard measures can be applied only during the transition period.[20]

A closer look at the text similarities existing in the RCEP and CPTPP also highlights the differences. For instance, the CPTPP Article 6.4, titled "Standards for a Transitional Safeguard Measure", provides for the time of application of a CPTPP safeguard that is clearly regulated and limited as follows:

1. *A Party shall maintain a transitional safeguard measure only for such period of time as may be necessary to prevent or remedy serious injury and to facilitate adjustment.*

2. *That period shall not exceed two years, except that the period may be extended by up to one year if the competent authority of the Party that applies the measure determines, in conformity with the procedures set out in Article 6.5 (Investigation Procedures and Transparency Requirements), that the transitional safeguard measure continues to be necessary to prevent or remedy serious injury and to facilitate adjustment.*

3. *No Party shall maintain a transitional safeguard measure beyond the expiration of the transition period.*

The corresponding RCEP article provides for the application of a transitional safeguard measure for a period not exceeding 3 years, which under exceptional circumstances can be extended to as much as 4 years.

In addition, Article 7.8 provides for a provisional RCEP safeguard measure that can be applied through a *"preliminary determination"* (rather than a full investigation) with a duration not exceeding 200 days. The CPTPP text does not include a similar provision.

Overall, comparison of the RCEP and CPTPP chapters on trade remedies, and especially the provisions on transitional safeguard measures, leaves the impression that the clear legal drafting of the CPTPP text is intended to provide certainty that the transitional safeguard measures are an exception. A reading the RCEP text does not leave the same impression. Instead, the drafting of the transitional RCEP safeguard measures appears to leave more discretion to investigating authorities and member states on the application and duration of these measures.

---

[20] In the CPTPP, a transition period relates to a particular good, and is the 3-year period beginning on the date of entry into force of the agreement, except where the tariff elimination for the good occurs over a longer time, in which case the transition period is the amount of time agreed for the staged tariff elimination of that good.

Part III
Trade in Services

7.   Trade in Services

Liberalization of trade in services is particularly relevant in Asia and the Pacific, where there is a striking divergence in the degree of market openness among the various RCEP member countries. According to the Services Trade Restrictiveness Index developed by the Organisation for Economic Co-operation and Development (OECD), Australia, Japan, the Republic of Korea, and New Zealand are RCEP's most open countries (in that order), with scores below the average level of restrictiveness among the 48 countries in the sample, as well as among the 37 OECD countries. By contrast, Indonesia, Thailand, the PRC, and Malaysia are the least open, as their scores figure above the sample average (Figure 14).

In assessing the potential and actual degree of trade liberalization triggered by RCEP, former attempts in the ASEAN context should also be taken into account. In spite of ASEAN ambitions to liberalize trade in services, the Services Trade Restrictiveness Index paints an unflattering picture of ASEAN's effective (i.e., applied) regulatory treatment of services.[21]

Notwithstanding successive ASEAN attempts to make trade in services more liberal than the commitments under other agreements—including the General Agreement on Trade in Services (GATS), the ASEAN Framework Agreement on Services, and some of ASEAN preferential trade agreements (PTAs) with Dialogue partners—considerable room still exists for deeper, competition-enhancing reforms in services markets after decades of negotiation and initiatives.

Mutual recognition agreements under the ASEAN framework, which are a key factor to implement services mobility, vary significantly in design, scope, and likely effectiveness, revealing marked sector-specific differences in the underlying political economy. Some of these mutual recognition agreements were mere hortatory frameworks for possible adoption, others were considerably more prescriptive.

On top of that, the proliferation of extra-regional PTAs of which RCEP is part and parcel—especially CPTPP and bilateral PTAs between individual ASEAN members and third countries from the OECD area—has generated significant ASEAN Framework Agreement on Services-plus commitments that do not flow back into ASEAN through an ASEAN Framework Agreement on Services MFN clause.

The scope and structure of Chapter 8 – Trade in Services in the RCEP Agreement virtually replicate those in AANZFTA and CPTPP, as the chapter includes provisions on national and MFN treatments, market access, local presence, and several other areas, which are listed in Table 9. These rules are subject to Parties' Schedules of Specific Commitments (Annex II) and Schedules of Reservations and Non-Conforming Measures (Annex III), i.e., measures that violate certain articles of the chapter.

---

[21]   For a history and assessment of ASEAN's services trade liberalization, see Neo, Sauvé, and Streho (2019).

Figure 14: Services Trade Restrictiveness Index, 2020
(averages)

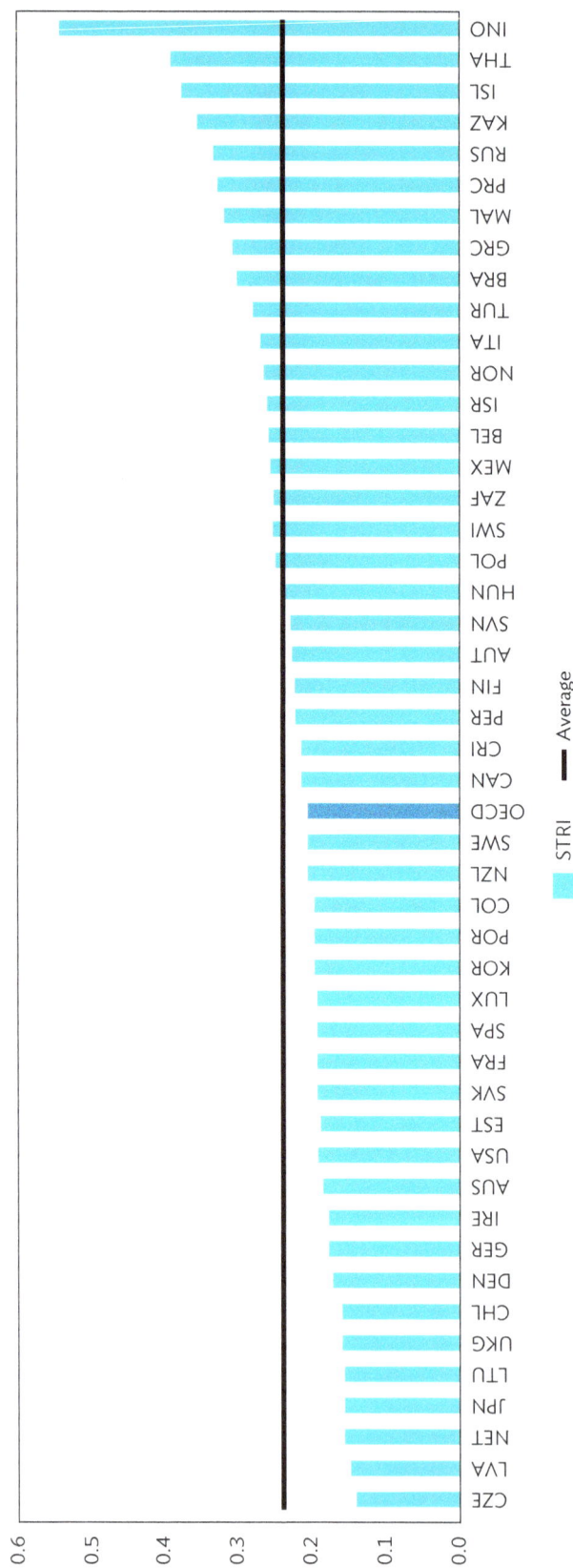

Legend: STRI, — Average

AUS = Australia; AUT = Austria; BEL = Belgium; BRA = Brazil; CAN = Canada; CHL = Chile; COL = Colombia; CRI = Costa Rica; CZE = Czech Republic; DEN = Denmark; EST = Estonia; FIN = Finland; FRA = France; GER = Germany; GRC = Greece; HUN = Hungary; INO = Indonesia; IRE = Ireland; ISL = Iceland; ISR = Israel; ITA= Italy; JPN = Japan; KAZ = Kazakhstan; KOR = Republic of Korea; LTU = Lithuania; LUX = Luxembourg; LVA = Latvia; MAL = Malaysia; MEX = Mexico; NET = Netherlands; NZL = New Zealand; NOR = Norway; OECD = Organisation for Economic Co-operation and Development; PER = Peru; POL = Poland; POR = Portugal; PRC = People's Republic of China; RUS = Russian Federation; SPA= Spain; STRI = OECD Services Trade Restrictiveness Index; SVK = Slovak Republic; SVN = Slovenia; SWE = Sweden; SWI = Switzerland; THA = Thailand; TUR = Turkey; UKG = United Kingdom; USA = United States; ZAF = South Africa.
Note: The STRI indices take values between 0 and 1, with 1 being the most restrictive. The STRI database records measures on a most favored nation basis. Air transport and road freight cover only commercial establishments (with accompanying movement of people). The indices are based on laws and regulations in force on 31 October 2020. The STRI regulatory database covers the 37 OECD countries, Brazil, the People's Republic of China, Costa Rica, Indonesia, Kazakhstan, Malaysia, Peru, the Russian Federation, South Africa, and Thailand.
Source: OECD STRI database. https://www.oecd.org/trade/topics/services-trade/documents/oecd-stri-policy-trends-2021.pdf (accessed October 2020).

In line with CPTPP, which was a pioneer in this field—but in contrast to the positive list approach taken by GATS and AANZFTA—Parties were required to schedule their commitments using the negative list approach, either on the date of entry into force or within a specified period after that date. Under this approach, all services are considered liberalized unless otherwise indicated through lists of reservations. This has the advantage of guaranteeing free trade for new services and providing easily identifiable targets for future negotiations.

Seven members (Australia, Brunei Darussalam, Indonesia, Japan, the Republic of Korea, Malaysia, and Singapore) decided to schedule their commitments through a negative list on entry into force. The remaining eight countries (Cambodia, the PRC, the Lao PDR, Myanmar, New Zealand, the Philippines, Thailand, and Viet Nam) have used a positive list—where only those services listed in their respective Schedules of Specific Commitments are open for RCEP services firms. Those countries, however, are required to switch to a negative list by 6 years after entry into force, except for the three least developed countries, for which the transitional period is extended to 12 years.

Bearing in mind the history of ASEAN trade in services agenda, it remains to be seen whether the RCEP built-in provisions for further liberalization will take place at a pace and timing leading to effective services liberalization.

Chapter 8 in the RCEP Agreement also provides three specific annexes on financial services (Annex 8A), telecommunications services (Annex 8B), and professional services (Annex 8C), with commitments and frameworks for enhanced cooperation. These annexes are examined in separate sections of this report.

Importantly, RCEP Chapter 8 includes several comprehensive measures to encourage increasing participation of least developed countries in regional trade in services. These measures provide a good opportunity for RCEP members and other partners to develop, together with the least developed countries, new initiatives for this purpose for example, under the Aid-for-Trade umbrella. In this regard, economic and technical cooperation (ECOTECH) is provided in RCEP Chapter 17 where capacity building and technical assistance are prioritized for developing and least developed countries.

Given these conditions, the relevant question is whether RCEP enshrines stronger and more coherent commitments for services trade liberalization than those in PTAs concluded by its members. Several factors need to be considered to answer this question, including those that do not bode well for the success of the Agreement:

(i)   Seven of the 15 RCEP Parties have joined CPTPP and so their mutual trade is already subject to RCEP rules that are virtually the same as CPTPP provisions. Furthermore, CPTPP commitments are rarely stronger than Parties' applied policies (Gootiiz and Mattoo 2017). This situation impacts on the incremental market access effect of RCEP.

(ii)   RCEP rules exacerbate, instead of improve, the complexity created by the 30 PTAs between RCEP members that are already in force or have been signed. RCEP services firms are thus confronted with an intricate grid of different sets of FTA rules governing their trade in the region, as was discussed in Section 1 and shown in Figures 1 and 2. Furthermore, the "noodle bowl" effect has been deepened by the participation of the most RCEP members in either CPTPP or FTAs with non-CPTPP parties, or both.

(iii)   Although RCEP's MFN provision is more progressive than in previous ASEAN FTAs (Table 9), it does not extend the benefits of previous market access concessions by a Party to the other Parties. Therefore, RCEP will not result, as some observers expect, in a coherent structure and a sort of rulebook with a single, user-friendly set of rules for the whole region (Tan et al. 2020).

That said, a number of positive factors can be taken into account in assessing possible outcomes of the Agreement, as presented below.

(i)   The complexity and intricacy of the region's services trade architecture, coupled with the long list of scheduled commitments and NCMs, makes it extremely difficult at this stage to measure the extent of the incremental market access that RCEP will bring about. However, it can be stated with some confidence that, because of the negative list schedules and increased market access in specific sectors, RCEP covers a greater share of overall trade in services between the Parties. As an example, Box 2 shows a list of new commitments that are expected to benefit services firms from Australia and New Zealand across an array of sectors. Presumably, this list also illustrates that other RCEP countries can expect similar benefits.

Box 2: Australia and New Zealand—Assessment on New Commitments by Other RCEP Countries

Both Australia and New Zealand already benefit from services commitments by other Regional Comprehensive Economic Partnership (RCEP) parties through existing plurilateral free trade agreements (FTAs), such as ASEAN–Australia–New Zealand Free Trade Area, CPTPP, and their respective bilateral FTAs with the People's Republic of China (PRC), Japan, and the Republic of Korea (which is linked only to Australia).

Official documents published in Australia and New Zealand have identified new market access commitments provided by many RCEP countries in a variety of sectors, as follows:

*   **Professional services** commitments from Cambodia, the PRC, Indonesia, the Republic of Korea, the Lao People's Democratic Republic (Lao PDR), Malaysia, Myanmar, the Philippines, and Thailand, including for legal, architectural, planning, engineering, veterinary, accounting, auditing, and bookkeeping services.

*   **Education services** commitments from the PRC, the Lao PDR, Myanmar, the Philippines, and Thailand, including for private secondary, higher, and adult education.

*   **Health care services** commitments from the PRC, Indonesia, the Lao PDR, Myanmar, and Thailand, covering private hospital ownership and operation, nursing, paramedicine, acupuncture, dentistry, and optometry.

*   **Other business services** commitments from the PRC, Indonesia, Malaysia, Myanmar, the Lao PDR, the Philippines, and Thailand, including for management consulting; advertising; executive search; specialty design; mining equipment, technology, and services; research and development; and real estate services.

Other new commitments have been identified in the following areas:

*   **Construction and related engineering services** (Indonesia, Malaysia, and Thailand)
*   **Tourism, recreational, cultural, and sporting services** (Malaysia and Thailand)
*   **Transport services** (the PRC, the Lao PDR, Malaysia, Myanmar, the Philippines, and Thailand)
*   **Wholesale trade services** (the Lao PDR, Malaysia, and Thailand)
*   **Retailing services, and franchising services** (the Lao PDR and Thailand)
*   **Computer-related services** (Indonesia, the Philippines, and Thailand)
*   **Environmental services** (the Philippines)

Sources: For Australia, DFAT (2020); for New Zealand, MFAT (2020).

(ii)   One of the most important, long-lasting benefits of RCEP in services is the adoption of the negative list format, which constitutes a continuous process of liberalization as new services are created, especially in the digital era, and do not require further negotiation. The full benefits of the negative list approach will only be reaped if and when all RCEP members adopt it. An encouraging development in this respect is that ASEAN has switched to the negative list approach in the next generation.

(iii) As with CPTPP, RCEP includes a ratchet mechanism under which any new liberalization measures autonomously adopted by a Party cannot be replaced by more restrictive provisions. This mechanism is expected to provide services suppliers with greater certainty in conducting business abroad.

Progress in services trade liberalization cannot be gauged only by examining RCEP's chapters and annexes devoted to trade in services. Several other chapters impinge on such liberalization and on growth in the region's trade, especially those dealing with investment, electronic commerce, and intellectual property. As an example, while the provisions of the chapter on trade in services deal with cross-border trade (GATS' Mode 1), sales through affiliates can be subject to rules of the Investment chapter. Furthermore, the Schedules of Reservations and Non-Conforming Measures cover services and investment together. Similarly, the protection of intellectual property rights (RCEP's Chapter 11) is especially important for a number of sectors, such as audiovisual services (including book publishing and sound recording) and computer-related services.

Finally, as many services are linked to trade in goods, either directly (as an example, transport services) or indirectly (for instance, advertising) provisions of RCEP's chapters dealing with this trade, including customs, ROO, SPS, NTBs, and the like (Chapters 2 to 7) are also relevant to ascertain the Agreement's overall impact on the region's services trade expansion.

Table 9: Trade in Services: Comparison of RCEP, AANZFTA, and CPTPP

	RCEP	AANZFTA	CPTPP
Definitions and scope	Includes services supplied through GATS' four modes. Exclusions: government procurement and services, subsidies and/or grants, cabotage in maritime transport; and air transport services.	Virtually same provisions; no mention of cabotage	Virtually same provisions; no mention of cabotage
National and MFN treatments	MFN more progressive than in the two FTAs but it does not extend the benefits of previous market access concessions by a Party to the other Parties.	Standard provisions	Standard provisions
Market access	No limitations on number of service suppliers, value and number of services transactions, or number of employees; maximum percentage on foreign shareholding or total value of individual or aggregate foreign investment.	Same language	Virtually same provisions
Local presence	Service suppliers should not be required to establish a local entity, office, or affiliate, or be resident in a territory to supply services there.	No provisions	Virtually same provisions
Domestic regulation	Licensing requirements should not be used to restrict the supply of services. Licensing fees and criteria should be objective and transparent.	Same provisions	Virtually same provisions

continued on the next page

Table 9 *continued*

	RCEP	AANZFTA	CPTPP
Recognition	Recognition of qualifications of foreign services suppliers by one Member should not imply recognition by any other Member. Recognition of qualifications should not be used to discrimination.	Similar provisions	Similar provisions
Denial of benefits	A Party may deny the benefit of this chapter to a service supplier of another Party, if that supplier is a juridical person owned or controlled by persons of a non-Party.	Similar provisions	Similar provisions
Transparency	Parties should publish promptly and make publicly available on the internet: (a) all relevant measures of general application affecting trade in services, (b) all relevant international agreements to which Parties are signatories, (c) Transparency List of existing measures that are inconsistent with national treatment and market access commitments.	Virtually same provisions; no Transparency List	Parties should maintain or establish appropriate mechanisms for responding to inquiries and they should provide advanced notice and opportunity for comment before regulations go into effect.
Payments and transfers	Except under the circumstances requiring measures to safeguard the balance of payments, a Party should not apply restrictions on international transfers or payments for current transactions and on any capital transaction inconsistently with its commitments.	Same provisions	Payments and transfers should be permitted to move freely across borders, and to be made in a usable currency at market exchange rates, but parties may regulate transfers in a way that is not discriminatory.
Ratchet mechanism	If any member autonomously liberalizes regulations or policies that allow foreign firms to supply services, that liberalization cannot be revoked later.	No provisions	Similar language
Increasing participation of least developed countries	This chapter should facilitate (a) strengthening least developed countries' domestic services capacity and their efficiency and competitiveness, among other things, through access to technology on a commercial basis, (b) improving their access to distribution channels and information networks, (c) liberalization of market access in sectors and modes of supply of export interest to them.	Same provisions	No provisions
	Least developed countries are not required to make commitments on MFN or Transparency List, nor to identify sectors or subsectors for future liberalization. They are allowed to submit Schedule of Specific Commitments within 12 years—instead of 6 years—after entry into force.	No provisions	

AANZFTA = ASEAN-Australia-New Zealand Free Trade Area, CPTPP = Comprehensive and Progressive Agreement for Trans-Pacific Partnership, FTA = free trade agreement, GATS = General Agreement on Trade in Services, MFN = most-favored nation, RCEP = Regional Comprehensive Economic Partnership.
Source: Authors.

8. Financial Services

Historically, the proliferation of FTAs with increasingly significant provisions on financial services over the past quarter century results from the groundbreaking General Agreement on Trade in Services (GATS) within WTO, followed by negotiations on a Trade In Services Agreement (TiSA) under the Doha Round, which were suspended in 2013. Meanwhile, both the United States (US) and the European Union (EU) were involved in negotiating several FTAs covering financial services, paving the way for wider coverage and deeper obligations in this area.

The influence of these two major trading partners over the shape and depth of financial liberalization over the globe is witnessed by their respective FTAs with the Republic of Korea, which are considered new templates for financial services rules. The US-Korea FTA of 2012 has been used as a prototype for drafting TPP and other FTAs, while the EU-Korea FTA of 2011 has served as a model for EU's more recent agreements, including those with other RCEP countries such as Japan and Singapore.

In drafting financial services provisions in FTAs, negotiators had to reconcile two conflicting objectives: financial liberalization and preserving the integrity and stability of the financial system through prudential safeguards. The different trade-offs and resulting weights of the two objectives explains many of the disparities among various agreements.

The RCEP's Annex 8A on financial services attempts to strike a balance between financial liberalization and prudential measures, but the latter appear to prevail over the former, in contrast to CPTPP. The annex sets out strong prudential safeguards that temper or qualify specific provisions favoring financial openness. Such provisions, which in any case are stronger than corresponding rules in the AANZFTA, involve the following:

(i)   More transparency and certainty for financial service suppliers in RCEP markets.

(ii)   Coverage of "new financial services", to accommodate financial innovation. New financial services are those that are not supplied in a given member country but are supplied and regulated in any other member country. This may apply to a service related to current and new products, or the manner in which a product is delivered.

(iii) Commitments to higher foreign equity caps than in the Parties' previous bilateral and plurilateral FTAs.

(iv)   The free transfer and processing of information.

One of the functions of the RCEP Joint Committee is to consider any proposal to amend the Agreement.[22] It is therefore useful to highlight the similarities and differences between this annex and the treatment of financial services in CPTPP.

---

[22] The RCEP Joint Committee, composed of senior officials designated by each RCEP Party, is established to consider any matter relating to the implementation and operation of the RCEP Agreement.

Similarities with CPTPP

(i)   Both FTAs link countries with drastically different financial systems and regulatory frameworks, inspired by Islamic principles, common law, or civil codes. There are also huge variations in the economies' degree of openness to global financial markets and foreign investment in the financial sector.

(ii)   RCEP and CPTPP include commitments that create opportunities for cross-border trade in financial services to increase and to help reduce regulatory restrictions on commercial presence: on financial firms established in, or looking to enter, their respective member countries. In both agreements, provisions on cross-border trade are far less frequent than those on commercial presence, through which financial services are typically traded.

(iii)   The two agreements share many general market access principles applicable to financial services—such as national treatment and most-favored nation—as well as specific clauses prohibiting (a) limitations on the number of financial institutions, the total value or number of their transactions, or the total number of people they employ; and (b) requirements on specific types of legal entity or joint venture through which a financial institution may supply a service.[23]

(iv)   Both FTAs include specific provisions to liberalize (a) trade in insurance, new financial services, portfolio management, settlement, and clearing services for financial assets; and (b) access to payment and clearing systems operated by public entities, and to official funding and refinancing facilities, except for lender of last resort (central bank) facilities.

(v)   In the two agreements, Parties are allowed to take measures for prudential reasons, including maintenance of the safety, soundness, integrity, or financial responsibility of individual financial institutions or financial service suppliers, as well as the safety and financial and operational integrity of payment and clearing systems. These prudential measures can be adopted or maintained for the protection of investors, depositors, policyholders, or persons to whom a fiduciary duty is owed by a financial service supplier.

(vi)   In both agreements, financial services are excluded from the prohibition of data localization measures contained in their e-commerce chapters. Although Parties are committed to allow financial institutions to transfer data and engage data processing services across national borders, a member country can require *"a financial service supplier in its territory to comply with its laws and regulations in relation to data management and storage and system maintenance, as well as to retain within its territory copies of records.[24]"*

Differences with CPTPP

(i)   ***Minimum standard of treatment (MST).*** The CPTPP is the first FTA applying MST to financial services. The MST obligation, which is absent from RCEP, provides financial institutions with "fair and equitable treatment", involving access to the courts and due process of law as well as "full protection and security" (adequate police protection), both in accordance with customary international law. This provision, which is included in the investment chapter, is expected to shield financial institutions from arbitrary and discriminatory actions by the

---

23   In the case of RCEP, these prohibitions appear in Chapter 8—Trade in Services, where they apply to all services.

24   Article 9.3 of "Transfers of Information and Processing of Information" in RCEP Chapter 8 – Trade in Services Annex 8A on Financial Services.

judicial system and police in the host country, and thus to stimulate services trade and foreign direct investment.

(ii) **Dispute settlement.** In contrast with RCEP, an investor-state dispute settlement mechanism is available in CPTPP for the enforcement of financial service suppliers' rights, including MST. However, if a financial institution challenges a regulation, it must request a joint, binding, determination by home and host financial authorities on whether the regulation has been taken for prudential reasons or not. As a result, a claimant de facto, needs to be supported by their own government, as a prerequisite for a successful dispute (Gelpern 2016). There are many other specific rules on establishment and procedures of panels and arbitration as well as qualifications of panelists and arbitrators.

(iii) **Transparency.** Under CPTPP, in developing a new regulation of general application, a Party may consider submissions by other Parties or their financial institutions with regard to the objectives and the potential effects of the proposed regulation.

(iv) **Specific sectoral provisions.** The CPTPP, spurred by the US, contains provisions regarding state-owned postal entities that play an important role in Asian financial markets, particularly in Japan, by selling insurance and other financial services.

In conclusion, the key differences between the two FTAs are in MST and dispute settlement. CPTPP's distinct provisions in these two areas strengthen the rights of foreign financial firms and therefore lowering barriers to entry in CPTPP financial markets.

9. Telecommunications Services

All ASEAN+1 FTAs contain an Annex on Telecommunications Services. Nevertheless, the scope of RCEP rules on this topic is much wider and the commitments are much stronger than others due to the heavy influence of CPTPP provisions. In the years preceding RCEP, those provisions also shaped discipline on telecommunications in the FTAs that some CPTPP countries had concluded with future RCEP members that were not in CPTPP, as in Australia's FTAs with the PRC, Indonesia, and the Republic of Korea.

The RCEP's Annex 8B on Telecommunication Services builds on existing ASEAN FTAs through these ways:

(i)   Recognizing the value of competitive markets to deliver a wide choice in the supply of telecommunications services and to enhance consumer welfare, and that regulatory needs and approaches differ market by market.

(ii)   Applying to measures affecting trade in public telecommunications services, including

   (a) measures relating to access to and use of public telecommunications networks or services.

   (b) measures relating to obligations regarding suppliers of public telecommunications networks or services.

(iii) Excluding measures affecting the cable or broadcast distribution of radio or television programming.

(iv)   Including disciplines on access and use of public telecommunications systems and access to essential telecommunications facilities.

(v)   Committing Parties to prevent anticompetitive practices.

Annex 8B replicates CPTPP's newest features and therefore is innovative in many respects as it:

(i)   extends procompetitive market access rules to mobile services, the fastest growing segment in telecommunications. This extension represents the key innovation in the annex.

(ii)   commits Parties to allow the portability of mobile telephone numbers and to cooperate to promote reasonable international mobile roaming rates.

(iii) includes provisions on flexibility in the choice of technology. Restrictions on technology, favoring domestic suppliers, have thwarted competition and use of new technologies. Reportedly, these new provisions can be a response to the stringent policies of some RCEP countries to protect their telecommunication sector from the PRC's supremacy in 5G technology.

(iv)   commits RCEP members to ensuring that suppliers of public telecommunications services will provide reasonable and non-discriminatory treatment for access to submarine cable systems.

(v)   contains obligations with regard to unbundling of network elements, and access to poles, ducts, and conduits.

Despite these significant innovations, the annex is expected to have little impact on market access, for two major reasons:

(i)   Among services sectors included in RCEP Parties' Schedules of Reservations and Non-Conforming Measures (NCM), telecommunications is typically included by all seven countries, both developed and developing, that have used the negative list approach. Likewise, countries in the positive list group have introduced strict market access limitations.

(ii)   Telecommunications is one of the least open sectors worldwide, as also shown by the extensive list of NCM in CPTPP. The seven RCEP countries that are also CPTPP members will experience very little change because the relevant provisions of the two agreements share strong similarities. Furthermore, CPTPP's rules on telecommunications have been used as a template in the bilateral FTAs some of these countries have concluded with other RCEP members that are not in CPTPP.

Notwithstanding these limitations, Australia has identified new market access opportunities stemming from commitments made by Indonesia, the Lao PDR, Malaysia, and Thailand. These openings should likely also benefit other RCEP countries.

More generally, the annex creates a broader, updated, and uniform framework of regulatory disciplines governing trade in public telecommunication services. This framework reflects new developments in approaches to regulation of markets since the conclusion of TPP. It is expected to enhance cooperation and trade among RCEP members, thus buttressing the backbone of the information and communications technology (ICT) infrastructure, which is crucial for the growth and sustainable development of Asia and the Pacific. In this respect, development cooperation could play a role. Sustainable development, especially in rural areas of least developed countries, may be promoted by a more extensive use of mobile phones at lower fixed and variable costs for consumers, with internet connections and related applications.

10. Professional Services

The Annex 8C on Professional Services provides an opportunity for members to lower behind-the-border barriers to professional services trade, by encouraging

(i)   dialogue and negotiations on mutual recognition of professional qualifications, licensing, or registration in professional services sectors of mutual interest; and

(ii)   development of mutually acceptable professional standards and criteria in such areas as education; examinations; experience; conduct and ethics; professional development and recertification; scope of practice; local knowledge; and consumer protection.

Although several services-related Mutual Recognition Agreements have been concluded under the ASEAN Framework Agreement Services (AFAS), inclusion of a separate annex on professional services is a novelty for six of the RCEP countries (Cambodia, the PRC, the Lao PDR, Myanmar, the Philippines, and Thailand).

Furthermore, greater market access for many professional services has resulted from specific new commitments in the schedules of Cambodia, the PRC, Indonesia, the Republic of Korea, the Lao PDR, Malaysia, the Philippines, and Thailand. These Parties' commitments will benefit firms that supply legal, architectural, planning, engineering, veterinary, accounting, auditing, and bookkeeping services (DFAT 2020).

The CPTPP includes a separate annex on professional services with far more detail than RCEP's one. It not only contains general provisions and specific commitments, including in engineering and architectural services, temporary licensing or registration of engineers, and legal services. It should be noted that, as with RCEP, mutual recognition agreements are optional, not compulsory.

An interesting feature of CPTPP's annex is the establishment of a Professional Services Working Group, which meets annually to support the activities of the relevant professional and regulatory bodies in pursuing activities related to mutual recognition and development of professional standards.

Part IV
Temporary Movement
of Natural Persons
and Investment

11. Temporary Movement of Natural Persons

The RCEP under Chapter 9 – Temporary Movement of Natural Persons (MNP) aims to facilitate movement of people on temporary basis engaged in trade in goods, supply of services, or conduct of investment. This is by ensuring efficient visa-processing procedures and transparency-related requirements for the application process. The coverage of the chapter is in effect limited to business persons.

Chapter 9 of RCEP comprises commitments on the following:

(i)   Business visitors, intracorporate transferees and other categories, as specified in each countries' Schedule of Specific Commitments, including length of stay and provisions for their spouses and dependents.

(ii) Transparent and expeditious processing of applications for temporary entry; ensuring that any fees imposed are reasonable in that they do not represent an unjustifiable impediment to MNP.

(iii) Enhanced transparency, including making publicly available explanatory materials on all relevant immigration formalities; maintaining mechanisms to respond to enquiries regarding laws and regulations affecting MNP.

The RCEP excludes measures affecting natural persons seeking work in a member country, also measures regarding nationality, citizenship, residence, or permanent employment. The rules included in this chapter and Parties' specific commitments are almost the same as those governing MNP in AANZFTA and other ASEAN+1 FTAs. Reportedly, Indonesia is the only RCEP country that will make improvements over GATS and AANZFTA on services supplied by natural persons (DFAT 2020). However, greater MNP liberalization can still be generated by the application of these rules and Parties' specific commitments to MNP between RCEP countries not linked through bilateral or plurilateral FTAs.

Compared with the RCEP MNP, the CPTPP provisions appear less liberal. CPTPP permits a country to refuse to follow immigration formality of a business visitor from another country if there is an ongoing labor dispute in the planned place of employment or if the business visitor is involved in an employment dispute.

However, unlike RCEP, CPTPP has established a Committee on Temporary Entry for Business Persons to review the state and challenges of implementing measures stipulated in the MNP chapter. The committee will explore ways to further facilitation temporary entry of business visitors, meeting every 3 years.

12. Investment

Foreign direct investment (FDI), the major component of assets covered in the RCEP investment chapter, plays an important role in RCEP's economies. In turn, these 15 economies account for 16% of the world's FDI stock and 24% of FDI inflows. However, intra-RCEP FDI flows represent 30% of total FDI in the RCEP region, which is a lower share than that of other important plurilateral FTAs.

Scope of Chapter Compared to CPTPP

The scope and depth of RCEP's investment provisions reflect the recent evolution of investment disciplines in RTAs going well beyond tariff reductions. In fact, commitments per Chapter 10 – Investment in the RCEP Agreement are very similar to those of RTAs concluded by ASEAN with its Dialogue Partners, which, in turn, were inspired by ASEAN Comprehensive Investment Agreement. However, major differences between RCEP and CPTPP are apparent, especially with regard to dispute settlement.

Looking closer at the RCEP text reveals certain characteristics. Investment is considered under a broad, "asset-based" definition that includes FDI, portfolio investment (shares, bonds), loans, and intellectual property rights (IPRs). However, unlike for CPTPP, the definition excludes derivative contracts. Chapter 10 covers investment liberalization, protection and dispute settlement arrangement.

Under investment liberalization, RCEP provides for MFN and national treatment as well as fair and equitable treatment both in the pre- and post-establishment phase of an FDI. It prohibits performance requirements with regard to forced transfer of technology, and forced adoption of a given rate or amount of royalty under a license contract. However, least developed countries are exempted from these two prohibitions.

Under investment protection, RCEP provides almost the same protection as in CPTPP with regard to transfer of funds, expropriation, and compensation. It clarifies the meaning of expropriation by distinguishing between direct and indirect expropriation and provides compensation for losses owing to armed conflict, civil strife, or state of emergency.

The dispute settlement provisions of RCEP and CPTPP differ significantly. In RCEP, there are no provisions for investor–state dispute settlement, although these are included in AANZFTA and in most current international investment agreements involving RCEP member countries. This investor–state dispute settlement is now used frequently in FTAs with investment provisions worldwide (see Table 10). However, RCEP contains a work program requiring member countries to enter discussions on this topic no later than 2 years after the Agreement's entry into force. Such discussions should be concluded within 3 years after they started. The work program is the result of a compromise stemming from New Zealand's opposition to investor–state dispute settlement (MFAT 2020).

Table 10: Investment Comparison of RCEP and CPTPP

	RCEP (Chapter 10)	CPTPP (Chapter 9)
Definitions and scope		
Investment definition	Covers direct and indirect investment, including shares, stocks, bonds, loans, rights in contracts, IPRs	Same provisions plus coverage of futures, options and other derivatives
Scope	Does not apply to government procurement; subsidies or grants; services supplied in the exercise of governmental authority neither on a commercial basis nor in competition with one or more service suppliers	Only specific paras do not apply to government procurement, export promotion, foreign aid programs.
Geographical scope	No provisions	Applies to central, regional, or local governments or authorities of Parties
Denial of benefits	These clauses prevent third country nationals who own or control the investor from gaining access to protection if their home country is not a Party	Same provisions
Investment liberalization	National treatment, MFN treatment, fair and equitable treatment and full protection and security, agreeing with the customary international law minimum standard of treatment of aliens	Same provisions plus (a)"fair and equitable treatment" includes the obligation not to deny justice in criminal, civil or administrative adjudicatory proceedings agreeing with the principle of due process embodied in the principal legal systems of the world; and (b) "full protection and security" requires each Party to provide the level of police protection required under customary international law.
Prohibition of performance requirements	Prohibits (a) local content requirements; (b) trade-balancing requirements; (c) foreign exchange restrictions; (d) export controls; (e) forced transfer of a particular technology, production process, or other proprietary knowledge; and (f) forced adoption of given rate or amount of royalty under a license contract. Prohibitions (e) and (f) do not apply to Cambodia, the Lao PDR, and Myanmar.	Virtually same provisions plus All prohibitions do not apply to Party from adopting or maintaining measures, including environmental measures: (i) necessary to secure compliance with laws and regulations that are not inconsistent with this Agreement; (ii) necessary to protect human, animal or plant life or health; or (iii) related to the conservation of living or non-living exhaustible natural resources.

continued on the next page

Table 10 *continued*

	RCEP (Chapter 10)	CPTPP (Chapter 9)
Investment protection Transfer of funds	Free transfer of funds relating to a covered investment, in any freely usable currency at the market rate of exchange prevailing at the time of transfer. Exceptions include: application laws and regulations relating to: (a) bankruptcy, insolvency, or the protection of the rights of creditors including employees; (b) issuing, trading, or dealing in securities, futures, options, or derivatives; and (c) taxation	Virtually same provisions
Expropriation	Direct and indirect expropriation admitted only for a public purpose, in a non-discriminatory manner and on payment of compensation. Non-discriminatory regulatory actions to achieve legitimate public welfare objectives, such as protection of public health, safety, public morals, the environment, and real estate price stabilization, do not constitute indirect expropriation (Annex 10B)	
Compensation	Compensation to be paid without delay, equivalent to the fair market value of the expropriated investment and to be effectively realizable and freely transferable. Compensation for losses owing to armed conflict, civil strife, or state of emergency is also provided.	
Investment promotion and facilitation	Non-compulsory provisions on investment promotion	Same provisions
Social provisions	No provisions	General provisions on corporate social responsibility and environmental, health, and other regulatory objectives
Dispute settlement	Work program establishing that the Parties should enter discussions on the settlement of investment disputes between a Party and an investor of another Party no later than 2 years after the Agreement's entry into force. Such discussions should be concluded within 3 years after they begin.	Dispute settlement provisions on consultation and negotiation; submission of a claim to arbitration under ICSID Convention or UNCITRAL Arbitration Rules; selection of arbitrators; conduct of arbitration; awards. However, several provisions have been suspended (Article 2) until Parties agree to end the suspension.

CPTPP = Comprehensive and Progressive Agreement for Trans-Pacific Partnership, ICSID = International Centre for Settlement of Investment Disputes, IPR = intellectual property right, Lao PDR = Lao People's Democratic Republic, MFN = most-favored nation, RCEP = Regional Comprehensive Economic Partnership, UNCITRAL = United Nations Commission on International Trade Law.
Source: Adapted from RCEP and CPTPP legal texts.

Although Chapter 10 of RCEP does not provide for a specific state-state dispute settlement, RCEP Chapter 19 – Dispute Settlement details a general mechanism under which investors can turn to their home state for support if they consider a host state has failed to meet its investment chapter obligations, which it can eventually result in a formal claim against the host state. However, this provision has an important caveat, which does not apply to pre-establishment rights, i.e., those relating to admission or approval of foreign investment. Because investor–state dispute settlement are absent and recourse to the state-to-state dispute settlement mechanism is possible, the investment chapter has been labeled as "A State-to-State WTO Style System for Now" (Ewing-Chow and Losari 2020).

By contrast, CPTPP, which has incorporated TPP's investment chapter in full, contains a comprehensive dispute settlement mechanism that includes provisions on consultation and negotiation; submission of a claim to arbitration under ICSID Convention or UNCITRAL Arbitration Rules; and selection of arbitrators, conduct of arbitration, and awards. These provisions are in line with those of recent FTAs, which very often cover both investor-state and state-state disputes (Table 10), while an appellate body is mentioned only as a future option.

However, with the withdrawal of the US turning TPP into a less ambitious CPTPP, several investment provisions have been suspended until participating countries agree to end the suspension (Article 2). This decision involves significant revisions and narrowing of commitments, and reportedly sets aside several issues that the US valued but other TPP countries did not: Goodman (2018) notes that "For example, in the CPTPP investment chapter, investors' ability to litigate disputes under investment agreements and investment authorizations—which are used mostly for mining and oil investments—will be more limited relative to TPP."

Table 10 summarizes the key features of RCEP's investment provisions and compares them with those of CPTPP, highlighting similarities and differences.

Figure 15: Share of Preferential Trade Agreements with Mechanism to Solve Disputes
(%)

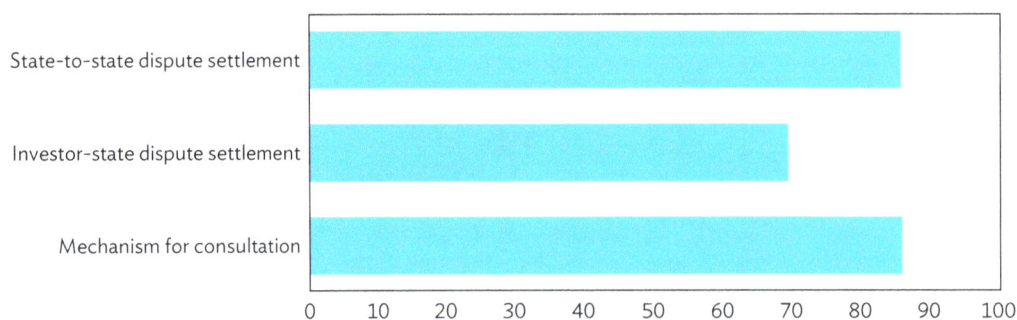

Source: Crawford and Kotschwar (2018).

Possible Impact

Several factors mean that the value added of the Investment Commitment in enhanced investment liberalization and protection is likely to be small. RCEP investors are already covered by international investment agreements and FTAs with investment provisions among countries. Examples include ASEAN Comprehensive Investment Agreement; AANZFTA; the ASEAN–PRC Investment Agreement; ASEAN–Korea Investment Agreement; and the PRC, Japan, and Korea Investment Agreement. Furthermore, Ewing-Chow and Losari (2020) report that "the RCEP investment chapter does not appear to offer advanced refinements to the standards contained in the Parties' existing international investment agreements so much as a compromise based on the lowest common denominators among the Parties."

The absence of investor–state dispute settlement is likely to push investors toward the use of investor–state dispute settlement in ASEAN Comprehensive Investment Agreement, AANZFTA, and a number of international investment agreements, rather than having to navigate the cumbersome state-state dispute settlement mechanism under RCEP.

Unlike the provisions on trade in services, from the start, all RCEP Parties chose the negative list approach to state their exemptions from the coverage of the chapter. Although the approach creates a framework for future liberalization efforts, the Schedules of Reservations and Non-Conforming Measures (where these exemptions are listed) are very long and apply to all Parties and many sectors. As an example, while for the first time the PRC has followed the negative list approach, its RCEP concessions do not exceed its level of current effective openness to foreign investment. For some industries, such as commercial vehicle manufacturing, the openness prescribed by the latest domestic laws exceeds RCEP's listed commitments (Tang and Wei 2020). Observers have described the RCEP investment provisions as a consolidation of existing conditions for market access in several bilateral agreements in the region (UNCTAD 2020).

By contrast, official documents issued by Australia and New Zealand state that these countries will benefit from new investment commitments, as are identified in Box 3. These are in addition to services trade commitments (illustrated in Box 2) that may generate investment in services sectors under Mode 3.[25]

It is also useful in this context to compare RCEP's market access commitments on investment to those agreed within CPTPP. Absent detailed examination of the two Schedules, some preliminary conclusions can be drawn from existing documentation. For example, Australia views CPTPP, together with its FTAs with Japan, the Republic of Korea, and Singapore, as a "higher ambition agreement" than RCEP. In particular, the market access commitments Brunei Darussalam and Malaysia made in their RCEP Schedules are more restrictive than what they had offered under CPTPP (Australia 2020). Furthermore, the PRC, which formally applied to join CPTPP in September 2021, reportedly would have to make greater concessions in both investment protection (such as the acceptance of investor–state dispute settlement) and investment liberalization (Crivelli and Inama 2022b). It is argued that even the enhanced market access commitments under the EU–China Comprehensive Agreement on Investment (CAI) fall short of the high CPTPP standards.

---

[25] Mode 3 of supplying services is defined in the WTO General Agreement on Trade in Services (GATS). It refers to the delivery of services through the commercial presence of service providers in the importing country. This could be a physical professional or business establishment, i.e., foreign direct investment.

Box 3: Australia and New Zealand—New Investment Commitments from RCEP Countries

Australia—The Regional Comprehensive Economic Partnership (RCEP) will be the first time that Australia receives investment commitments from Cambodia, the People's Republic of China (PRC), the Lao People's Democratic Republic (Lao PDR), the Philippines, and Thailand, covering, to varying degrees, manufacturing, mining, forestry and agriculture, and portfolio investment.

People's Republic of China—The nation's RCEP commitments essentially mirror domestic reforms, removing restrictions on grains processing (soybean, rice, flour, corn, and sugar), exploitation of gold, silver, platinum and lithium, and manufacture of rail transit equipment, among others.

Philippines—With the exception of most favored nation (MFN) status, the Philippines' commitments are close to what it gave members of the Association of Southeast Asian Nations (ASEAN) in the ASEAN Comprehensive Investment Agreement. Manufacturing commitments are reasonable, and will be of some commercial value to Australia.

Thailand—Commitments in agriculture (cattle farming) and manufacturing (including food processing) are commercially meaningful to Australia. Although mining commitments are still very limited, Thailand has now committed MFN on mining investment.

Cambodia and the Lao PDR—Allowing for their least developed country status, these nations have tabled reasonable offers in RCEP that will improve the transparency and predictability of regulation in mining and manufacturing. Nevertheless, their market access commitments are limited, particularly from Cambodia.

New Zealand—New commitments by some RCEP Parties go beyond existing free trade agreements and will be of benefit. In particular, the PRC and ASEAN countries that are not party to the Comprehensive and Progressive Agreement for Trans-Pacific Partnership will be making investment market access commitments to New Zealand for the first time.

Sources: Excerpts from Australia DFAT (2020) and New Zealand MFAT (2020).

In sum, while RCEP is expected to generate positive effects on investment protection and market access, despite all the examined limitations, the provisions in other chapters of the Agreement—such as those for trade in goods and services, intellectual property, and e-commerce—could stimulate more investment than the specific investment provisions (UNCTAD 2020).

Part V
Cross-Cutting Regulatory Issues

13. Intellectual Property Rights

Chapter 11 – Intellectual Property in the RCEP Agreement shows significant improvement in commitments when compared to the treatment of the same issue in ASEAN+1 FTAs. This can be observed in the number of pages devoted to the cooperation measure.[26]

Intellectual property cooperation covers the standard set of areas enshrined in the Trade-Related Aspects of Intellectual Property Rights (TRIPS) Agreement: copyright and related rights, trademarks, geographical indications, industrial designs, patents, layout of integrated circuits, protection of plant varieties and undisclosed information. It does so with varying degrees of detail and includes new areas covering genetic resources, traditional knowledge, and folklore.

A Regional Intellectual Property Rights Protection Framework

Building on TRIPS Agreement provisions, RCEP has created a regional framework for protecting and enforcing intellectual property rights (IPRs) by harmonizing and aligning procedures and standards for their protection and enforcement. This is a major undertaking in Asia and the Pacific, given that extremely different IPR regimes characterize the region. RCEP commits participating countries to ratify or accede to several key multilateral agreements for the protection of IPRs, including those on patents, copyright, and trademarks. It has provided guidelines to streamline the establishment of some IPRs, such as those relating to electronic filing of applications and making information available online, which will reduce regulatory and business compliance costs. RCEP has affirmed the right for Parties to use fully the flexibilities recognized in the Doha Declaration on the TRIPS Agreement and Public Health and urged countries to promote transparency in intellectual property regimes, making it easier for traders to obtain information about their rights. It encouraged information sharing, cooperation, and capacity building between member economies.

The most distinct feature of IPR discipline in RCEP is its emphasis on a balanced and inclusive approach, which tries to reconcile *"the rights of intellectual property right holders and the legitimate interests of users and the public interest.*[27]*"* This is observed throughout the chapter's stated objective being that *"the protection and enforcement of intellectual property rights should contribute to the promotion of technological innovation and to the transfer and dissemination of technology, to the mutual advantage of producers and users of technological knowledge and in a manner conducive to social and economic welfare, and to a balance of rights and obligations.*[28]*"* Chapter 11 provisions require that member countries adopt measures to prevent rights holders from abusing IPRs or resorting to practices that may restrain trade or hinder the international transfer of technology. It also stipulates that enforcement procedures

---

[26] The RCEP devotes 44 pages to intellectual property, while AANZFTA devotes only four pages. In the ASEAN-PRC FTA, intellectual property cooperation appears in the Memorandum of Understanding. CPTPP devotes 75 pages to this discussion.

[27] Article 11.1.1 (c) of "Objectives" in RCEP Chapter 11 – Intellectual Property.

[28] Article 11.1.2 of "Objectives" in RCEP Chapter 11 – Intellectual Property.

should be applied in a way that avoids creating trade barriers, while concurrently safeguarding against abuse. The RCEP extends the "fair use" exception to include not only copyright but also trademarks.[29]

For the first time in an FTA, RCEP has allowed member countries to establish measures to protect genetic resources, traditional knowledge, and folklore (traditional cultural expression). This provision grants governments policy space and flexibility when dealing with these topics and is a manifestation of the inclusive character of the chapter. The chapter is accompanied by Annex 11A containing special, unique provisions for least developed countries. The annex lists their technical assistance requests, together with Viet Nam's, particularly covering an electronic application system for processing, registering, and maintaining trademarks. RCEP also provides least developed countries with transitional periods of as much as 15 years, compared to 3–5 years for the other countries. All these rules are additional expressions of RCEP's inclusive approach to intellectual property rights.

The RCEP intellectual property chapter compares well with CPTPP and aligns with the growing importance of the digital economy. The "fair use" exception clause in RCEP is the same as the CPTPP, including for copyright and trademarks. As with CPTPP, RCEP talks about technological protection measures and enforcement, criminal procedures against unauthorized activities, enforcement procedures on intellectual property infringement, and rules of cooperation on cross-border measures such as eliminating international trade in pirated and counterfeit goods. RCEP also adds commitments around Geographical Indications,[30] including adopting or maintaining due process and transparency obligations in respect to any regime they provide for their protection. This provision means that a Party can challenge the protection of a name as a Geographical Indication in another Party if it is known to consumers as the common descriptive term for the relevant good. In such case, producers of those goods will not be prevented from using what is considered as a common name. Furthermore, in a situation where a Party is required under an international agreement to protect specific names, interested persons—such as producers in RCEP countries—would have the opportunity to comment on whether those names should be protected. These provisions are less ambitious than the ones in FTAs concluded by the EU with RCEP members Japan, Malaysia, Singapore, and Viet Nam.

Possible Impact

The impact of the intellectual property provisions on member countries will depend on four key factors: (i) the extent to which intellectual property legislation has evolved in a given RCEP country, and how far it is from the RCEP requirements; (ii) enforcement integrity of the relevant laws and regulations in a country; (iii) country's participation in other FTAs, particularly with advanced economies (CPTPP or EU FTAs where intellectual property provisions are similar to RCEP or more stringent); and (iv) the duration and coverage of the implementation of the agreed provisions in the chapter.

---

[29] According to Section 107 of the US Copyright Act, the fair use of a copyrighted work, including such use by reproduction in copies or phonorecords or by any other means specified by that section, for purposes such as criticism, comment, news reporting, teaching (including multiple copies for classroom use), scholarship, or research, is not an infringement of copyright.

[30] A geographical indication is a sign used on products that have a specific geographical origin and possess qualities or a reputation that are due to that origin. In order to function as a geographical indication, a sign must identify a product as originating in a given place (World Intellectual Property Organization).

One may conclude from these four factors that the seven RCEP countries that are also part of CPTPP (Australia, Brunei Darussalam, Japan, Malaysia, New Zealand, Singapore, and Viet Nam) will benefit marginally. However, as trading partners they will benefit from the eventual improvements in the intellectual property regimes of the remaining eight countries. It should be noted that the other eight countries (Cambodia, the PRC, Indonesia, the Republic of Korea, the Lao PDR, Myanmar, the Philippines, and Thailand) differ widely in evolution of their intellectual property infrastructure, with the Republic of Korea and the least developed countries at the two extremes of the spectrum. In principle, the least developed countries will benefit the most, provided their legislation and enforcement mechanism are upgraded to meet RCEP requirements. Technical assistance and development financing will play a key role in this respect.

An interesting case in point is the PRC, whose intellectual property enforcement is closely watched and criticized by its trading partners, especially the US and the European Union. The law firm Baker McKenzie, in examining the possible impact of RCEP's intellectual property provisions on the PRC, concluded that "[T]he RCEP would have some positive, albeit limited, effects on intellectual property protection in the PRC. What is probably more interesting to see is how RCEP will impact the enforcement of the revised/new intellectual property laws in the PRC..., and the further alignment of intellectual property protection at the regional level" (Baker McKenzie 2020).

The conclusion that RCEP impacts intellectual property protection and enforcement differently is based on most commitments of the PRC in the RCEP's chapter having already been implemented—or being implemented, as is the case for the protection of electronic rights management information. Also, although the chapter's enforcement section mostly replicates relevant TRIPS Agreement provisions, member countries are subject to more stringent obligations on the destruction of pirated copyright goods and counterfeit trademark goods. The PRC has already incorporated corresponding provisions in its copyright and trademark laws. However, the RCEP provisions are viewed as "welcome additions" to intellectual property protection and enforcement because, in practice, courts in the PRC do not in general issue orders for the destruction of the infringing goods, materials, and implements.

Another possible effect of RCEP on intellectual property enforcement in the PRC relates to government's use of software. The chapter commits member countries to maintain laws, regulations, or policies that provide for their central government to use only non-infringing computer software and to encourage regional and local governments to adopt or maintain similar measures. Although the PRC enacted corresponding Administrative Measures in 2013, the commitments under RCEP will compel its central and local governments to follow such measures more strictly.

14. Electronic Commerce

Chapter 12 – Electronic Commerce in the RCEP Agreement has three objectives: promoting electronic commerce among RCEP member countries, building an ecosystem of trust in the use of e-commerce, and enhancing cooperation among stakeholders for its development. The provisions apply to all measures affecting trade by electronic means. This broadly includes transmissions of data, information, and digital products over the internet or over private electronic networks. Transmissions by financial services firms are excluded from the chapter and separately dealt in Annex 8A on financial services of RCEP Chapter 8 – Trade in Services.

Scope of the Chapter

The scope and depth of the chapter are in line with "new generation" regional trade agreements (RTAs). It tackles issues across four areas:

(i)   **Trade facilitation.** Paperless trading, electronic authentication, and signing.

(ii) **Creating a conducive environment for e-commerce**. Protection of online consumers and personal information, unsolicited commercial electronic messages, domestic regulatory framework, transparency, and cybersecurity.

(iii) **Customs duties.** The current practice of not imposing customs duties on electronic transmissions is maintained, in line with the WTO Ministerial Decision.

(iv) **Promoting cross-border e-commerce**. Location of computing facilities and cross-border transfer of information by electronic means.

For 5 years after the Agreement enters into force, Cambodia, the Lao PDR, and Myanmar, as least developed countries, are exempted from many of RCEP's provisions in three of the four areas identified above, with customs duties being the exception.

RCEP versus CPTPP

The e-commerce provisions in Chapter 12 of RCEP were influenced by those embodied into TPP and then reproduced, with no changes, in CPTPP. According to many observers, e-commerce and other digital trade-related provisions were *"the most transformative measures"* in the whole TPP (United States International Trade Commission 2016, p. 353).

As shown in Table 11, most provisions are similar or identical across RCEP and CPTPP. However, there are several critical differences. The most important disparities between the two agreements concern the rules on data flows and localization, which firms providing computer services consider to be fundamental. They argue, in fact, that stringent disciplines against "digital protectionism" would allow firms to locate computer servers and data storage anywhere, based only on cost, efficiency, and security, and so reducing trade costs.

(i) **Rules on data flows.** Also known as cross-border transfer of information by electronic means, these are the most contentious in regional and multilateral negotiations on digital trade. In line with CPTPP, RCEP provides free data flows. However, it contains broader and significant exceptions, such as measures to achieve public policy objectives and those for protection of essential security interests. Equally important, such measures cannot be disputed by other member countries. Therefore, there is no room for complaint against infringements of the chapter.

(ii) **Rules on data localization** (or data storage requirements) are again less stringent in RCEP, which allows for much wider policy space. In fact, as an exception to the prohibition on data localization, a member country can impose any measure *"necessary for the protection of its essential security interests,"* making clear that the *"legitimate public policy objective"* exception can be decided solely by the implementing Party.[31]

Despite these limitations, the data flows and localization commitments are the first of this kind for a number of RCEP countries, improving on the corresponding articles in the ASEAN Agreement on Electronic Commerce and ASEAN+1 FTAs.

Other significant discrepancies between RCEP and CPTPP are the following:

(i) **Provisions on personal information protection.** These are less comprehensive in RCEP, which requires member countries to adopt or maintain a legal framework for this purpose, but it does not include important clauses such as those on non-discriminatory practices in protecting users of electronic commerce and on measures to promote compatibility of different regimes, such as recognition of regulatory outcomes.

(ii) **Issues related to source code**. The source code is the fundamental, human-readable component of a software.[32] Issues related to source code are not addressed in RCEP. Conversely, CPTPP prohibits the forced transfer of, or access to, source code of software owned by a person of another member country, as a condition for the import, distribution, sale or use of such software, or of products containing it. This clause has become rather controversial. In fact, countries favoring that discipline aim to protect the interests of their industries, while promoting innovation. By contrast, some others, mostly developing countries, maintain that this prohibition would jeopardize the transfer of technological know-how (UNCTAD 2021).

(iii) **Dispute settlement.** In RCEP, the Electronic Commerce chapter is not at present subject to Dispute Settlement, and the general review of the Agreement will review the application of Dispute Settlement to this chapter. By contrast, CPTPP's dispute settlement provisions are applicable to the corresponding chapter.

Looking to the Future

Overall, RCEP provisions are not as comprehensive nor as strict as in CPTPP. However, using a second-best approach and a forward-looking perspective, experts note in Honey (2021, p. 227) that "there are still reasons to welcome the RCEP provisions in their contribution to regional data governance, foremost among which is that PRC is a member of the Agreement.... The PRC has usually taken a very different approach on data than the CPTPP model. By contrast, in RCEP, the PRC has agreed

---

[31] Article 12.14.3 (a) and (b) of "Location of Computing Facilities" in RCEP Chapter 12 – Electronic Commerce.
[32] Microsoft Office is an example of a proprietary source code.

that the default should be free flows of data and no forced data localization, though with a potentially broad exceptions provision. Even if in practice the exceptions become the binding constraint, RCEP nevertheless creates a forum for an ongoing conversation on data flows, data localization, source code and the treatment of digital products in a formal Dialogue on Electronic Commerce among the Parties. This dialogue may eventually help to narrow the scope of exceptions (and hence potential impediments to digital trade) in the future."

In fact, RCEP has provided a useful platform to discuss not only "current and emerging issues" (Box 4) and other broader "matters relevant to the development and use of electronic commerce" (Article 12.16).

Box 4: Dialogue on Electronic Commerce (Article 12.16)

The Parties recognize the value of dialogue, including with stakeholders where appropriate, in promoting the development and use of electronic commerce. In conducting such a dialogue, the Parties shall consider the following matters:

- Cooperation agreeing with Article 12.4 (Cooperation).
- Current and emerging issues, such as the treatment of digital products, source code, and cross-border data flow and the location of computing facilities in financial services.
- Other matters relevant to the development and use of electronic commerce, such as anticompetitive practices, online dispute resolution, and the promotion of skills relevant for electronic commerce including for cross-border temporary movement of professionals.

Source: Chapter 12 in Global Policy Development Center. RCEP: Goods Market Access Implications for ASEAN. https://www.mti.gov. sg/-/media/MTI/Microsites/RCEP/All-Chapters-and-Market-Access-Annexes/Chapter-Text/Chapter-12.pdf.

Under these conditions, in visualizing different scenarios concerning the evolution of RCEP's provisions, it is relevant to analyze some most recent agreements, involving several RCEP members, which have tried to increase market access and the benefits of digital trade, and at the same time to locate electronic commerce in a broader socioeconomic context. This strategy could be instrumental in reconciling business interests with the wider sociopolitical objectives emerging from a multistakeholder approach, involving shared responsibility between governments, technology service providers, and users.

Such agreements are the Digital Economy Partnership Agreement (DEPA) involving New Zealand, Singapore, and Chile and the Digital Economy Agreement (DEA), an amendment to the Singapore–Australia FTA of 2015. Both DEPA and DEA, both signed in 2020, are much broader in scope than RCEP and CPTTP, as shown in Figure 16. In fact, the new agreements touch upon a great variety of subjects, ranging from social issues such as the inclusion of indigenous communities, women, and rural populations, support for SMEs, and encouraging access to the internet and a safe online environment; the most advanced topics in digital innovation, such as artificial intelligence and fintech; and more traditional issues such as government procurement, competition, and capacity building.

The Dialogue on Electronic Commerce as a forum not only can pave the way for negotiations on the issues outlined above and to forge a common position among RCEP members on the ongoing Joint Statement Initiative (JSI) under the WTO umbrella (Box 5), in which some RCEP countries are leading participants, could result in a multilateral or plurilateral agreement on digital trade within the WTO.

Box 5: The Joint Statement Initiative on E-commerce

The Joint Statement Initiative on E-commerce negotiations were launched in 2019. The Regional Comprehensive Economic Partnership (RCEP) is well represented as the co-conveners of the Initiative are Australia, Japan, and Singapore, which along with two other RCEP members—the Republic of Korea and New Zealand—have led technical discussions in plenary or small groups. The number of participants in the initiative has grown to 86 World Trade Organization members, accounting for more than 90% of global trade and representing all major geographical regions and levels of development.

The negotiations have made encouraging progress even amid the challenges presented by the coronavirus disease pandemic. The current consolidated negotiating text covers members' proposals on the following themes: enabling electronic commerce; openness and e-commerce; trust and e-commerce; cross-cutting issues; telecommunications; market access; and scope and general provisions.

Source: World Trade Organization.

Table 11: Comparison of Digital Trade Provisions in CPTPP and RCEP

Digital Trade Provisions	CPTPP 2016–2018	RCEP 2019
No customs duties on electronic transmissions	Y	Y
Non-discrimination on digital products	Y	N
Domestic electronic transactions framework	Y	Y-
Personal information protection	Y	Y--
Electronic authentication or signatures	Y	Y
Online consumer protection	Y	Y
Paperless trading	Y	Y
Express shipments	Y	in FTA
Electronic invoicing	N	N
Electronic payments	N	N
Data flow	Y	Y--
Data localization	Y	Y--
Data localization for financial services	N	N
Unsolicited commercial e-messages	Y	Y
Cooperation	Y	Y
Cooperation on competition policy	N	N
Cybersecurity	Y	Y
Dispute settlement	Y	N
Transparency	N	Y
Source code	Y	N

CPTPP = Comprehensive and Progressive Agreement for Trans-Pacific Partnership, FTA = free trade agreement, RCEP = Regional Comprehensive Economic Partnership.
Notes: Y means provision is similar or identical across agreements from the CPTPP "baseline"; Y- means provision is less comprehensive and/or ambitious; Y-- means provision is far less comprehensive and/or ambitious; and N means no similar provision included.
Source: Adapted from Honey (2021).

Figure 16: Topic Coverage in CPTPP, RCEP, DEPA, and DEA

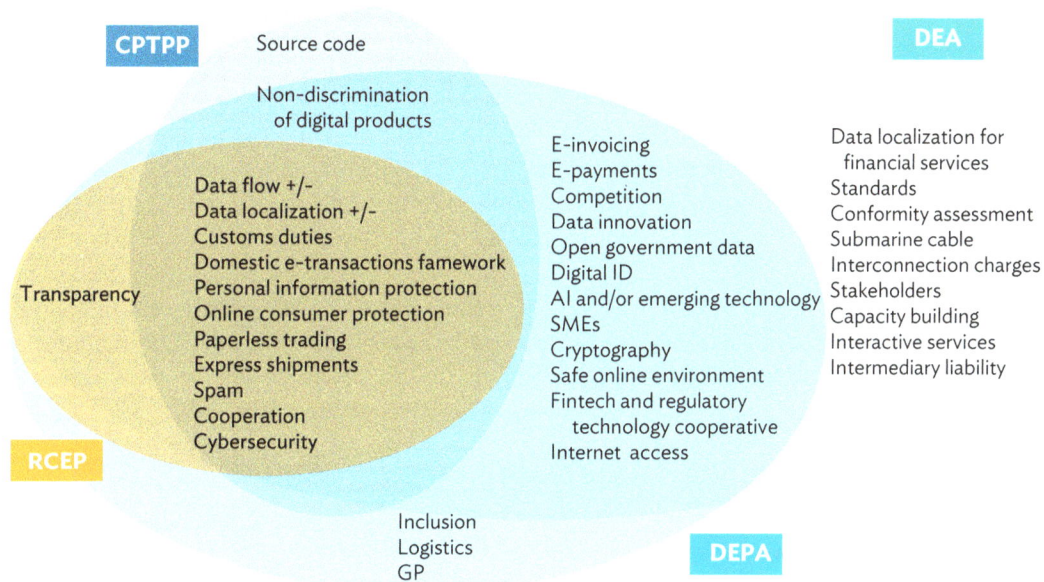

CPTPP

DEA

Source code

Non-discrimination
of digital products

E-invoicing
E-payments
Competition
Data innovation
Open government data
Digital ID
AI and/or emerging technology
SMEs
Cryptography
Safe online environment
Fintech and regulatory
  technology cooperative
Internet access

Data localization for
  financial services
Standards
Conformity assessment
Submarine cable
Interconnection charges
Stakeholders
Capacity building
Interactive services
Intermediary liability

Data flow +/-
Data localization +/-
Customs duties
Domestic e-transactions famework
Personal information protection
Online consumer protection
Paperless trading
Express shipments
Spam
Cooperation
Cybersecurity

Transparency

RCEP

Inclusion
Logistics
GP

DEPA

AI = artificial intelligence, CPTPP = Comprehensive and Progressive Agreement for Trans-Pacific Partnership, DEA = Digital Economy
Agreement, DEPA = Digital Economy Partnership Agreement, fintech = financial technology, GP = government procurement,
ID = identification, RCEP = Regional Comprehensive Economic Partnership, SMEs = small and medium-sized enterprises.
Source: Honey (2021).

15. Competition

The RCEP's competition provisions reflect Parties' growing awareness of the importance of competition law and policy, including their crucial links with trade policy, and at the same time recognition of the significant differences in the capacity and national regimes of RCEP countries.

Over the past few years, considerable progress has been achieved in promoting and implementing competition legislation in Asia and the Pacific, particularly within RCEP's developing countries. In fact, all ASEAN nations have enacted economywide competition laws since 2015. However, despite these juridical advances, law enforcement is lax in many RCEP countries, especially in least developed countries and other developing countries.

The recent progress in national legislations has translated into much deeper competition law and policy provisions in RCEP than those appearing in ASEAN+1 FTAs. For example, the ASEAN-Australia-New Zealand FTA (AANZFTA), which is considered as among the most advanced in that category, deals only with cooperation between countries and clearly specifies that: *"Nothing in this [Competition] Chapter requires a Party to develop specific competition related measures to address anticompetitive practices, or prevents a Party from adopting policies in other fields, for example to promote economic development.*[33]*"

By contrast, Chapter 13 – Competition in the RCEP Agreement includes obligations for member countries to adopt or maintain competition laws and regulations that prohibit anticompetitive activities and to establish or maintain authorities to implement its competition laws. That said, it recognizes that each country has a sovereign right to enforce its own competition laws and policies and allows for exclusion or exemptions based on public policy or public interest. Each country is also obliged to apply its competition laws and regulations to all entities engaged in commercial activities, regardless of ownership.

This important clause implies an extended coverage of the chapter, which includes not only private and state-owned enterprises (SOEs), but also covers consumer protection with obligations to adopt or maintain domestic laws and regulations to ban misleading practices, or false or misleading descriptions in trade. This improves consumer redress mechanisms.

In addition to the "hard-law" obligations in the areas of competition law and policy and consumer protection, Chapter 13 contains "soft-law" provisions where Parties only "may" undertake or "recognize" specific activities or issues, with no obligations to take action. This language appears used to accommodate the different degree of sophistication of competition law and policy implemented in RCEP countries. As an example, *"[e]ach Party recognizes the importance of timeliness in the handling of competition cases.*[34]*"* Furthermore, *"[e]ach Party also recognizes the importance of improving awareness of, and access to, consumer redress mechanisms.*[35]*"*

---

[33] Article 1.4 of "Basic Principles" in AANZFTA Chapter 14 – Competition.
[34] Article 13.3.11 of "Appropriate Measures against Anti-Competitive Activities" in RCEP Chapter 13 – Competition.
[35] Article 13.7.3 of "Consumer Protection" in RCEP Chapter 13 – Competition.

Special transitional provisions are included for least developed countries and Brunei Darussalam, which should comply with the obligations relating to measures against anticompetitive activities within 5 years after the Agreement's entry into force.

In CPTPP, competition law and policy is covered in two separate chapters:

- Chapter 16, which is almost similar in coverage to the competition provisions of Chapter 13. These two chapters are compared in Table 12.

- Chapter 17, which is devoted to SOEs and designated monopolies.

Table 12: Competition Chapter: Comparison between RCEP and CPTPP

	RCEP	CPTPP
Objectives	To promote competition in markets, and enhance economic efficiency and consumer welfare through the adoption and maintenance of laws and regulations to proscribe anti- competitive activities, and through regional cooperation on the development and implementation of competition laws and regulations among the Parties	Very similar language, although there is no separate clause on objectives
Coverage	No definition of anticompetitive activities, only a footnote "Examples may include anticompetitive agreements, abuses of a dominant position, and anticompetitive mergers and acquisitions"	No definition nor examples
	Each Party shall apply its competition laws and regulations to all entities engaged in commercial activities, regardless of their ownership	No provisions but separate chapter on state-owned enterprises
Procedural fairness in competition law enforcement	No provisions	Rules providing the right to counsel, a reasonable opportunity to be heard and to present evidence, the right to offer expert analysis, the right to cross-examine any testifying witness, and the right to appeal and/or seek review
Private rights of action	No provisions	Each Party should adopt or maintain laws or other measures that provide an independent private right of action, defined as the right of a person to seek redress, including injunctive, monetary or other remedies, from a court or other independent tribunal for injury to that person's business or property caused by a violation of national competition laws, either independently or following a finding of violation by a national competition authority

continued on the next page

Table 12 *continued*

	RCEP	CPTPP
Consumer protection	Each Party shall adopt or maintain laws or regulations to proscribe the use in trade of misleading practices, or false or misleading descriptions	Similar language but with definition of fraudulent and deceptive commercial activities and examples
	Each Party also recognizes the importance of improving awareness of, and access to, consumer redress mechanisms	No provision
Transparency	Any exclusion or exemption from the application of each Party's competition laws and regulations shall be transparent	A Party shall make available to the requesting Party public information concerning: (a) its competition law enforcement policies and practices; and (b) exemptions and immunities to its national competition laws
	Each Party shall make publicly available its competition laws and regulations, and any guidelines issued in relation to the administration of such laws and regulations	Each Party shall ensure that a final decision finding a violation of its national competition laws is made in writing and sets out, in non-criminal matters, findings of fact and the reasoning, including legal and, if applicable, economic analysis, on which the decision is based
	Each Party shall make public the grounds for any final decision or order to impose a sanction or remedy under its competition laws and regulations, and any appeal therefrom, subject to: (a) its laws and regulations; its need to safeguard confidential information; or its need to safeguard information on grounds of public policy or public interest; and (b) redactions from the final decision or order on any of the grounds referred to in (a)	Each Party shall further ensure that a final decision referred to above and any order implementing that decision are published, or if publication is not practicable, are otherwise made available to the public in a manner that enables interested persons and other Parties to become acquainted with them
Dispute settlement	Non-application	Same provision

CPTPP = Comprehensive and Progressive Agreement for Trans-Pacific Partnership, RCEP = Regional Comprehensive Economic Partnership.
Source: Authors' compilation.

Table 12 shows that the two chapters share some similarities. For instance, they both do not define anticompetitive activities, although RCEP lists several illustrative examples, such as anticompetitive agreements, abuses of a dominant position, and anticompetitive mergers and acquisitions. The absence of definition, however, is not considered a weakness, but rather "as much a strategic choice as a tactical one" in Gadbaw (2016, p. 86), where the author argues that within TPP negotiations, in which the US played a dominant role, "US regulators see significant risks in articulating standards when countries have already implemented them in domestic law" in the competition law and policy field of continuous and rapid evolution of concepts and practices.

Major differences between the two agreements are also apparent. The absence of an RCEP provision on the private right of action is among the most conspicuous differences, as it denies, as defined by CPTPP, *"the right of a person to seek redress, including injunctive, monetary or other remedies, from a court or other independent tribunal for injury to that person's business or property caused by a violation of national competition laws.*[36]*"*

---

[36]   Article 16.3.1 of "Private Rights of Action" in CPTPP Chapter 16 – Competition.

More generally, CPTPP's provisions are much deeper, involving obligations related to private rights of action and other critical areas such as transparency and procedural fairness in competition law enforcement. These are the topics where, besides the SOE chapter, CPTPP and its predecessor, the TPP, set groundbreaking rules inspired by the work of OECD and the International Competition Network.

Looking into CPTPP's Chapter 17 on SOEs, the same commentator maintains that *"Chapter 17 represents a more revolutionary approach to rule making than the more modest evolutionary approach of the competition chapter [16] .... Chapter 17 represents a critically important development in trade law and a major accomplishment of the TPP.... Chapter 17 signals a new strategy to discipline SOEs through trade law commitments as distinct from antitrust principles"* (Gadbaw 2016, pp. 82, 86). TPP and CPTPP include rules on SOEs not yet incorporated into other FTAs. While Malaysia and Viet Nam are the only two (CP) TPP countries with a large state-owned sector and have obtained a transitional preferential treatment, Chapter 17 appears to have been drafted having in mind the PRC's potential membership.

The CPTPP's SOE chapter provides broad coverage of SOEs that are principally engaged in commercial activity including those operating under delegated authority. The chapter includes commitments to ensure that SOEs make commercial purchases and sales based on commercial considerations, except for the provision of public services. Governments also agreed to ensure that their SOEs or designated monopolies do not discriminate against the enterprises, goods, and services of other Parties. The SOE chapter also includes obligations requiring Parties to provide their courts with jurisdiction over commercial activities of foreign SOEs so that one operating in a TPP country cannot claim sovereign immunity. Finally, Parties are required not to cause injury to another Party's domestic industry by providing non-commercial assistance (such as subsidies) to an SOE that produces and sells goods in the territory of another Party.

Within these innovative and strict rules on SOEs, which are far more ambitious than WTO's provisions, CPTPP's Chapter 17 allows for significant leeway through exemptions for sovereign wealth funds, export credit agencies, subcentral SOEs, those under an annual revenue ceiling of SDR 200,000 ($278,780 at 24 November 2021 conversion rate), and those in which the Party (i) directly owns up to 50% of the share capital; (ii) controls up to 50% of the voting rights; or (iii) does not hold the power to appoint a majority of members of the board of directors.

16. Small and Medium-Sized Enterprises

In entering global trade, small and medium-sized enterprises (SMEs), especially in developing countries and least developed countries, face disproportionate barriers, such as complex paperwork, stringent regulations, inefficient customs administrations, and expensive and slow delivery of small consignments. At the same time, the increasing speed of information and communication technology (ICT) and logistics makes it relatively easy and cheaper for the same set of SMEs to sell their goods and services around the world.

Chapter 14 – Small and Medium Enterprises in the RCEP Agreement is fully focused on issues specific to SMEs. Its objective is *"to promote information sharing and cooperation in increasing the ability of SMEs to use and benefit from the opportunities created by this Agreement.[37]"* However, other RCEP chapters, such as Chapter 12 – Electronic Commerce, and Chapter 4 – Customs Procedures and Trade Facilitation, also address SME issues.

Although Chapter 14 belongs to the soft-law category, it shows many areas for cooperation among the participating members are possible. These include encouraging e-commerce use, promoting awareness, understanding, and effective use of the intellectual property system; and sharing best practices on enhancing the capability and competitiveness of SMEs.

Unlike the equivalent CPTPP chapter, RCEP does not encourage each member economy to create a website to provide SMEs with easily accessible information on the Agreement and ways to use it. This initiative could be considered by the RCEP's Committee on Sustainable Development, dealing both with SMEs and economic and technical cooperation (Box 6).

In conclusion, while many RCEP provisions help SMEs, key benefits are expected to come from lowered tariff and nontariff barriers, increased market access for service providers, and trade facilitation rather than the exclusive chapter devoted to SMEs.

[37] Article 14.1.1 (c) of "Objectives" in RCEP Chapter 14 – Small and Medium Enterprises.

Box 6: Subsidiary Bodies of the RCEP Joint Committee

The Parties hereby establish an RCEP Joint Committee consisting of senior officials designated by each Party.... The RCEP Joint Committee shall meet within 1 year of the date of entry into force of this *Agreement and prior to the first meeting of the RCEP Ministers, and every year thereafter unless the Parties agree otherwise....*

The RCEP Joint Committee shall establish at its first meeting:
(a) a Committee on Goods, to cover work on trade in goods; rules of origin; customs procedures and trade facilitation; sanitary and phytosanitary measures; standards, technical regulations, and conformity assessment procedures; and trade remedies;
(b) a Committee on Services and Investment, to cover work on trade in services including financial services, telecommunication services, and professional services; temporary movement of natural persons; and investment;
(c) a Committee on Sustainable Growth, to cover work on small and medium enterprises; economic and technical cooperation; and emerging issues; and
(d) a Committee on the Business Environment, to cover work on intellectual property; electronic commerce; competition; and government procurement.

RCEP = Regional Comprehensive Economic Partnership.
Source: Chapter 18 – Institutional Provisions.

17. Economic and Technical Cooperation

The RCEP is not only the largest FTA in the world by population and total gross national product and the most diverse in different stages of development of its member countries—as witnessed by their income per capita levels. Out of the 15 members, six (Australia, Brunei Darussalam, Japan, the Republic of Korea, New Zealand, and Singapore) are classified by the World Bank as high-income economies (those with 2019 income per capita of $12,536 or more); four (the PRC, Indonesia, Malaysia, and Thailand) as upper middle-income economies (income per capita between $4,046 and $12,535); and the remaining five (Cambodia, the Lao PDR, Myanmar, the Philippines, and Viet Nam) in the lower-middle-income category (income per capita between $1,036 and $4,045). Cambodia, the Lao PDR, and Myanmar also belong to the United Nations (UN) group of least developed countries. Although there are no low-income countries (those with income per capita of $1,035 or less) among members, their striking income disparities are epitomized by the fact that the average income of Singaporeans (about $62,000) is more than 38 times higher than that of Cambodian citizens (roughly $1,600).

Narrowing Gaps, Maximizing Benefits

Chapter 15 - Economic and Technical Cooperation (ECOTECH) in the RCEP Agreement aims at narrowing such development gaps, while maximizing mutual benefits among the member economies, by inviting them to undertake ECOTECH activities that focus on trade in goods, trade in services, investment, intellectual property, e-commerce, competition, and SMEs, among others. Noticeably, trade facilitation and procurement do not appear in this list.

Priority is said to be given to activities benefitting developing and least developed countries that increase public awareness, and that enhance business access to information, accounting for the different levels of development and national capacity of each member and specific constraints faced by least developed countries. Presumably, in that context, developing countries are those that are categorized as per the UN classification, which includes high-income countries as well, such as Brunei Darussalam, the Republic of Korea, and Singapore.

The chapter prescribes that ECOTECH should support those activities that are trade or investment related as specified in the work program, which should be developed taking into consideration the provisions in this Agreement and needs identified by committees established under Chapter 18 – Institutional Provisions, which were identified in Box 6. The Committee on Sustainable Growth is the most suitable group for this purpose, as it covers work on ECOTECH as well as SMEs and emerging issues.

Resources for ECOTECH will be provided voluntarily. The countries may consider cooperation with, and contribution from non-members; or with subregional, regional, or international organizations and institutions.

By contrast, the corresponding ECOTECH chapter in CPTPP identifies a broader range of activities including those in areas not specifically related to trade, such as agriculture, industry, and services sectors, the promotion of education, culture and gender equality, and disaster risk management, among others.

18. Government Procurement

The provisions in Chapter 16 – Government Procurement of RCEP are the shortest and most modest of the whole Agreement, in both scope and depth. The provisions only apply to procurement implemented by central government entities, and so exclude subnational government bodies and state-owned enterprises. The chapter includes only procurement that is "expressly open to international competition" and is in accordance with generally accepted government procurement principles.

Scope of the Chapter

The focus of the chapter is limited to transparency and cooperation. On transparency, the only obligation is for the member countries to make procurement laws and regulations publicly available, while the other provisions—publicity of procurement procedures, availability of information by electronic means and in English—are on best-endeavor character. On cooperation, there are again only best-endeavor clauses on exchange of information on member countries' respective disciplines and in particular on best practices and electronic procurement systems. With regard to training, technical assistance, and capacity building, it is noted that although procurement obligations do not apply to the three least developed countries they can benefit from cooperation among the participating countries. Furthermore, procurement provisions are excluded from the Agreement's dispute settlement mechanism. Despite these severe limitations, however, Chapter 16 provides for a review every 5 years aimed at improvements to enable government procurement.

Comparison with CPTPP and WTO's Government Procurement Agreement

Observers following RTAs took the view that the depth and coverage of the procurement chapter in RCEP is rather limited. Government procurement was added to negotiations only in 2017, 4 years after negotiations began. One of the reasons for the delay and, therefore, for the modest scope of the chapter, was that no ASEAN+1 FTA included a chapter on government procurement. More importantly, the PRC has not yet committed to obligations in its bilateral or plurilateral agreements. However, in FTAs with Australia and New Zealand, the PRC accepted to negotiate market access on government procurement after completion of its long-standing, and still ongoing, negotiations to accede to WTO's Government Procurement Agreement (GPA).

Looking to developments in RCEP's coverage of procurement, the PRC's significant progress in GPA negotiations is important. Its latest 2019 offer is by far the most generous since 2007, although the other partners are yet to accept. If the PRC finally joins GPA, it could start a dialogue on government procurement within RCEP, supported by the other five RCEP countries that are already GPA members (Australia, Japan, the Republic of Korea, New Zealand, and Singapore). This initiative would be instrumental in preparation of the review of this chapter, which is scheduled for 5 years after the Agreement enters into force. Furthermore, the five current GPA members, together with other three

RCEP countries (Brunei Darussalam, Malaysia, Viet Nam) have also joined CPTPP and so are subject to its procurement provisions.

In sum, out of the 15 RCEP nations, eight are already committed to much wider and deeper obligations under either GPA or CPTPP or both. This overlap indicates that RCEP cannot function as a regional regulatory framework at its current state, and its contribution toward further liberalization of government procurement can still be elevated. In view of the this, a comparison of the procurement provisions in CPTPP and GPA (Table 13) is useful.

Table 13 : Government Procurement—Comparison of CPTPP and GPA

	CPTPP (Article 15)	GPA
Scope	• Government procurement of (a) good, service or any combination thereof; (b) by any contractual means, including: purchase; rental or lease, with or without an option to buy; BOT contracts and public works concessions contracts. • Procuring entities include central government, subcentral government and other entities. • The commitments apply only to procurement that each country has agreed to cover in its Schedule. • Exceptions: procurement necessary to protect public morals, order or safety; human, animal, or plant life or health, including environmental measures; intellectual property; or relating to the good or service of a person with disabilities, of philanthropic or not-for-profit institutions, or of prison labor.	• Similar provisions, with no mention of BOT contracts
General principles	• National and MFN treatments. • Timely and complete information. • Fair and transparent procedures. • Non-discriminatory and flexible technical specifications. • Compliance with laws regarding international labor rights is admitted.	• Similar provisions, but no mention of international labor rights

Special and differential treatment for developing countries and least developed countries	• Parties may agree to the delayed application of any obligation in this chapter, other than the MFN treatment principles by the developing country Party while that Party implements the obligation. The implementation period shall be only the period necessary to implement the obligation.
	• Developing countries may adopt or maintain transitional, non-discriminatory measures regarding:
	  • price preference program favoring domestic producers
	  • offset, i.e., condition requiring use of domestic content or similar action
	  • phased-in addition of specific entities or sectors.
	• Higher threshold than its permanent one.
		• Same treatment for developing countries, plus 3-year limit for implementation period
		• Same treatment for least developed countries, which are not singled out in CPTPP, allowing them a 5-year implementation period
		• Same treatment for developing and least developed countries

continued on the next page

Table 13 *continued*

	CPTPP (Article 15)	GPA
Procurement practices	• Conditions for participation. • Qualification and deadlines for suppliers. • Tender information. • Limited tendering. • Treatment of tenders and awarding of contracts. • Post-award information. • Ensuring integrity.	
Institutional measures	• Establishment by each Party of a domestic review authority that is independent of its procuring entities to review, in a non-discriminatory, timely, transparent and effective manner, a complaint by a supplier. • Establishment of Committee on Government Procurement to address matters related to the implementation and operation of this chapter, such as (a) cooperation between the Parties; (b) facilitation of participation by SMEs; (c) use of transitional measures; and (d) consideration of further negotiations, which should start no later than 3 years after the Agreement's entry into force.	• Similar provisions • The Committee on Government Procurement has broader functions, including adoption of work programs for the following items: collection and dissemination of statistical data; treatment of sustainable procurement; safety standards in international procurement.

BOT = built-operate-teansfer, CPTPP = Comprehensive and Progressive Agreement for Trans-Pacific Partnership, GPA = government procurement agreement, MFN = most favored nation, SMEs = small and medium-sized enterprises.
Source: Authors' compilation.

In conclusion, the procurement provisions are very similar in the two agreements, although procurement practices are more up-to-date in CPTPP, which includes build-operate-transfer (BOT) contracts. However, in the context of the RCEP membership with a most developing countries, of which three are least developed countries, the GPA provisions appear to be more in consonance with future amendments to Chapter 16 – Government Procurement in the RCEP Agreement. In fact, GPA grants special and differential treatment to least developed countries and contains no provisions regarding international labor rights, an issue that can be divisive, in light of the position of a number of RCEP developing countries, including the PRC, in this respect.

Part VI
Conclusion and Way Forward

19. Conclusion and Way Forward

The RCEP came into practice beginning 1 January 2022, following national ratification of the Agreement by six ASEAN and four non-ASEAN countries in early November 2021. Effective and timely implementation of the Agreement is key to its success. The RCEP text does propose establishment of a secretariat to monitor the progress in implementation, but its role and resources need to be clearly delineated.

The main findings of this report are organized around four elements: (i) incremental value: RCEP compared to CPTPP, WTO, and ASEAN+1 FTAs; (ii) implementation: challenges and policy proposals; (iii) built-in agenda and proposed amendments; and (iv) policy suggestions.

Trade in Goods

Incremental value

Several commentators and analysts expect that one of the major gains of RCEP derives from bringing under one common umbrella the existing panoply of FTAs in Asia and the Pacific. The preliminary analysis in this report casts some doubt on the expectations, taking into account: (i) the complexity of the tariff schedules, (ii) the long phasing-out calendars, (iii) the extensive use of differentiated offers and the administration of tariff differential, and (iv) the administration mechanisms of tariff quota.

A more complete and detailed analysis, matching the different tariff offers with trade flows and comparing them with CPTPP and other existing FTAs, is necessary to assess more precisely the potential value added of RCEP. Yet the complexity of the analysis reveals challenges the private sector may encounter in effectively using the preferential margin provided by RCEP with respect of the existing agreements.

Implementation

Several challenges are related to implementation of tariff schedules that depend on the ratification of individual RCEP members states and potential issues arising from the application of HS versions of the tariff phaseout schedules and related concordances.

Built-in agenda

Article 2.5, titled "Acceleration of tariff commitments" provides a built-in mechanism that should be used at the earliest opportunity to accelerate and simplify tariff commitments, thus providing further momentum to the RCEP Agreement.

Policy suggestion

There is ample scope for fact-based analysis of RCEP to help member states identify gaps in implementation and to provide policy options for addressing them. As for the built-in agenda, new tariff commitments could also account for the product composition of global value chains and eventually be linked to liberalization of related services. It is necessary to establish a public database permitting and facilitating online access for the private sector and researchers of the tariff lines phaseout under RCEP and other existing FTAs. This website should be updated constantly with the help of member states and the RCEP secretariat.

Rules of Origin

Incremental value

As for trade in goods, there are great expectations for RCEP ROO as trade facilitating factors and for supporting existing regional value chains. Undoubtedly, cumulation under RCEP has potential for such an outcome. However, the preliminary assessment of this report has identified potential obstacles deriving from (i) the limitation of the form of cumulation that excludes the possibility of full cumulation, (ii) the existence of tariff differentials and cumbersome provisions that are different across member states, (iii) the existence of different forms of certification of origin leading to different practices in member states during implementation, and (iv) the non-incorporation in RCEP text of best practices such as a non-alteration clause on documentary evidence of direct shipment.

A preliminary comparison of RCEP and CPTPP ROO text shows that CPTPP incorporates some of the best practices that have evolved from recent experience in administering ROO, such as self-certification. In comparison, RCEP is more hesitant in embracing such best practices. The major incremental value of RCEP is cumulation. Yet, as indicated, critical factors might hamper its effective utilization.

Implementation

The implementation of complex ROO is one of the reasons for low utilization of existing FTAs in the region. Several implementation challenges may arise from the possibility of adopting different origin certification systems and different interpretations of some provisions of Chapter 3 – Rules of Origin. RCEP will be facing several implementation challenges that could be addressed through a technical assistance program for government officials and private sector.

Built-in agenda

In recognition of the compromises reached to finish negotiations and the need for further refining the ROO, several clauses in Chapter 3 – Rules of Origin provide for a built-in agenda to review cumulation, certification, and ancillary provisions. This built-in agenda should be activated and finalized as soon as possible, imparting clarity and predictability to the rules of the origin chapter.

Policy suggestion

Research and studies should be carried out to present policy options and measures to further improve ROO and related certification requirements by adopting best practices, and so avoid repeating past pitfalls. These studies and research should be used as bases for the built-in intergovernmental mechanisms provided to improve RCEP's ROO. As for tariffs, a database and user interface should be established as soon as possible to provide accessible information on product-specific ROO and related certification procedures for the private sector, including product-specific rules of origin (PSROs) of existing FTAs to allow a fair comparison and the choice of the best route. A mechanism should be established to notify trade data on utilization of trade preferences and a related dataset should be established to monitor the effective utilization of trade preferences.

Customs Procedures and Trade Facilitation

Incremental value

There are two "WTO-plus" topics on which, RCEP goes farther than TFA's ambitions, although using hortatory language: (i) RCEP calls for customs clearance of goods within 48 hours of arrival. For express consignments, the time limit is reduced to six hours; and (ii) RCEP contains improved advance ruling provisions and a time limit of 150 days for the issuance of advance rulings. RCEP also contains two "CPTPP-plus" provisions: A 6-hour limit on customs clearance of perishable goods, and Parties may opt for a longer period for the full implementation of their commitments.

Implementation

Cambodia, the Lao PDR, Myanmar, and Viet Nam are allowed to postpone full implementation by 2–5 years. The most frequent subjects for delaying implementation are advance rulings, release of goods, application of information technology, trade facilitation measures for authorized operators, and risk management.

Policy suggestion

A number of measures are worth the consideration of the Committee on Goods, the subsidiary body of the RCEP Joint Committee in charge of trade facilitation: mandating members to use a single entry point and to employ World Customs Organization standards by a given deadline, introducing de minimis rules, allowing imports below a given monetary value to enter member countries duty-free.

Regional and multilateral technical cooperation and capacity building as well as financial assistance could be instrumental in helping Cambodia, the Lao PDR, and Viet Nam, in their implementation process.

Sanitary and Phytosanitary Measures and Technical Barriers to Trade

Incremental value

The RCEP nurtured expectations, especially in ASEAN least developed countries and also in Australia and New Zealand, to further gain market access on agricultural products and processed foodstuffs in PRC market. Such access, besides tariffs that are mostly being reduced or completely liberalized under previous bilateral FTAs, is mainly regulated by SPS requirements. Considered under this perspective, there is little incremental value in RCEP compared with existing WTO agreements on SPS and TBT and based on preliminary analysis of corresponding provisions in CPTPP. Overall, CPTPP contains greater language predictability, additional protocol on TBT on specific sectors, indicating the commitment of the Parties to greater convergence on TBT and SPS. As against this, the RCEP chapters on SPS (Chapter 5) and TBT do not contain a mechanism that may progressively reduce the incidence of nontariff measures (NTMs) in this area.

Implementation

There is no implementation agenda as the RCEP text is merely a replication of WTO commitments in the respective agreements. Implementation may be measured by assessing the initiatives that may be undertaken under the existing commitments of the SPS and TBT WTO agreements reiterated and articulated in the RCEP SPS and TBT chapters.

Built-in agenda

One of the striking factors of RCEP's regional integration ambitions and the incidence of NTM in the region is the absence of a built-in agenda in these critical areas. Importantly, and in comparison to CPTPP, RCEP does not provide for the establishment of an SPS nor a TBT committee to take the agenda forward and to provide a forum where experts of such a highly technical discipline could take steps to further facilitate the elimination of NTMs related to SPS and TBT requirements.

Policy suggestion

There is a need for further policy research to advocate mechanism to address NTMs arising from SPS and TBT requirements and regulations. Robust evidence exists that NTMs related to SPS and TBT requirements are creating impediments to trade beyond tariffs. Yet, there are no papers or mechanisms providing policy makers with actionable road maps on how to resolve them.

Trade Remedies

Incremental value

The trade remedies chapters in both RCEP and CPTPP mainly restate the use of such remedies according to the respective WTO agreements on safeguards, anti-dumping, and subsidies and countervailing measures. Both RCEP and CPTPP contain few additional provisions concerning notification and consultation in initiation of trade remedies.

Some RCEP members use trade remedies to a much larger extent than other RCEP partners and countries outside the region.

Emphasis in the RCEP text on transitional safeguard measures may cast doubt over the predictability of the tariff phaseout schedule as it contains wording and flexibility that gives leeway to those RCEP partners that may seek recourse to such measures.

Implementation

The implementation of the reduction of tariff commitments may cause increased recourse to trade remedies and the transitional safeguard clause. Therefore, use of trade remedies during the transitional phase needs to be monitored.

Built-in agenda

There is no built-in agenda in RCEP nor in CPTPP on trade remedies.

Policy suggestion

Few studies are dedicated to assessing the trend in the use of trade remedies in the region, their impact and causes, and an increased caseload in disputes brought to WTO Dispute Settlement Understanding. Given this, a study would be necessary to better understand the trade and economic consequences of any rising use of trade remedies in regional integration.

Trade in Services

Incremental value

As a result of the negative list schedules adopted by all members through different timelines and increased market access in specific sectors, RCEP covers a greater share of overall trade in services between the Parties, despite the overlapping provisions in CPTPP and ASEAN+1 FTAs. New market access opportunities have been identified in a variety of sectors, including educational services, health services, computer-related services, other business services, in the PRC, Indonesia, the Philippines, Thailand, and among other countries. However, a deep comparative analysis of schedules of commitments and non-conforming measures is yet to be conducted.

Implementation

Seven countries (Australia, Brunei Darussalam, Japan, the Republic of Korea, Malaysia, Singapore, and Indonesia) will apply the negative list on entry into force; five countries (the PRC, New Zealand, the Philippines, Thailand, and Viet Nam) will do so within 6 years later, while for the three least developed countries (Cambodia, the Lao PDR, and Myanmar), the transitional period has been extended to 12 years. The Committee on Services and Investment may establish or amend procedures for the modification or withdrawal of a Party's commitments in its Schedule of Specific Commitments or the conduct of arbitration.

Built-in agenda

The Parties shall review (i) the incorporation of safeguard measures pending any further developments in the multilateral fora pursuant to Article X of GATS (Article 8.21); and (ii) the issue of disciplines on subsidies related to trade in services in light of any disciplines agreed under Article XV of GATS to their incorporation into Chapter 8 – Trade in Services (Article 8.22).

Policy suggestion

A deep comparative analysis of schedules of commitments and non-conforming measures is necessary. The three least developed countries, and possibly other lower middle-income countries, would need technical assistance and capacity building to switch from the positive to the negative list.

Financial Services

Incremental value

Compared to ASEAN+1 FTAs, higher foreign equity caps in some commitments and coverage of "new financial services".

Telecommunications Services

Incremental value

Compared to ASEAN+1 FTAs, coverage of mobile services, including number portability and provisions on flexibility in the choice of technology. New market access opportunities stemming from the commitments made by Indonesia, the Lao PDR, Malaysia, and Thailand.

Policy suggestions for both

Proposed financial assistance to least developed countries for promoting more extensive use of mobile phones with internet connections in rural areas.

Professional Services

Incremental value

New commitments resulting in greater market access by Cambodia, the PRC, Indonesia, the Republic of Korea, the Lao PDR, Malaysia, the Philippines, and Thailand. These commitments would benefit firms supplying legal, architectural, planning, engineering, veterinary, accounting, auditing, and bookkeeping services.

Implementation

Establishment of a professional services working group to support professional and regulatory bodies in mutual recognition and developing professional standards.

Temporary Movement of Natural Persons

Incremental value

In Indonesia, greater market access over GATS and AANZFTA on services supplied by business persons.

Built-in agenda

No built-in-agenda.

Policy suggestion

As with CPTPP, this report proposes establishment of the Committee on Temporary Entry for Business Persons to (i) review the implementation and operation of this chapter, and (ii) consider opportunities for the Parties to further facilitate temporary entry of business persons.

Investment

Incremental value

(i) Adoption by all Parties of negative list approach on entry into force. (ii) "TRIMS-plus" prohibition of performance requirements extended to forced transfer of a particular technology, production process, or other proprietary knowledge as well as forced adoption of given rate or amount of royalty under a license contract. These new prohibitions do not apply to least developed countries. (iii) Greater market access mostly resulting from the alignment of RCEP commitments with those under CPTPP.

Built-in agenda

Work program requiring Parties to enter discussions on investor-state dispute settlement no later than 2 years after the Agreement's entry into force. Such discussions should be concluded by 3 years after they begin.

Policy suggestion

Least developed countries get 70% to 90% of their FDI flows from other RCEP countries. Economic and technical cooperation from these home countries, although not specifically mentioned in this chapter, could bolster least developed countries' position as recipients of FDI and other capital flows.

Intellectual Property

Incremental value

"TRIPS-plus": Coverage of genetic resources, traditional knowledge and folklore. "CPTPP-plus": Extension of the "fair use" exception to include not only copyright but also trademarks.

Implementation

Members are generally provided with a transitional period of 3–5 years, extended up to 15 years for the least developed countries among them.

Policy suggestion

Chapter 11 – Intellectual Property is accompanied by an annex containing special, unique provisions for least developed countries and Viet Nam. The annex lists their technical assistance requests. All least developed countries are asking, among other things, for support in setting up an electronic application system for processing, registering, and maintaining trademarks. Economic and technical assistance going well beyond what least developed countries request can play a key role in upgrading their IPR legislation and enforcement.

Electronic Commerce

Incremental value

Provisions on data flows and localization are the first of this kind for non-CPTPP members, and go beyond the commitments in FTAs between RCEP countries and the ASEAN Agreement on Electronic Commerce.

Implementation

(i) A Dialogue on Electronic Commerce within the RCEP Joint Committee. This forum could contribute to forging a common position for RCEP members within WTO's Joint Statement Initiative on E-commerce (JSI); and build convergence on social issues (inclusion, SMEs, internet access, a safe online environment) and on the most advanced topics in digital innovation, such as artificial intelligence and fintech.

(ii) The least developed countries (and in few instances, Viet Nam) are not obliged to apply several provisions for 5 years after entry into force.

Built-in agenda

Chapter 12 – Electronic Commerce is not at present subject to dispute settlement. As part of any general review of the Agreement, the Parties should review the application of dispute settlement to this chapter.

Policy suggestion

Economic and technical cooperation could assist least developed countries and Viet Nam in their implementation efforts.

Competition

Incremental value

The RCEP has much deeper provisions compared to ASEAN+1 FTAs. Parties are required to adopt or maintain competition laws and regulations that prohibit anticompetitive activities and to establish or maintain authorities for implementing its competition laws. Each Party is also obliged to apply its competition laws and regulations to all entities engaged in commercial activities, regardless of ownership.

Implementation

Least developed countries and Brunei Darussalam are allowed to comply with the obligations relating to measures against anticompetitive activities within 5 years after entry into force.

Policy suggestion

Technical assistance, including capacity-building activities, may play an important role in least developed countries' implementation phase.

Small and Medium-Sized Enterprises

Incremental value

This is the first FTA involving all ASEAN countries to include a separate chapter on issues specific to SMEs. Chapter 14 of RCEP requires that member countries share complete information about RCEP online and include links to other information for SMEs' doing business in the RCEP region.

Implementation

Following the CPTPP's example, the Committee on Sustainable Development, dealing both with SMEs and economic and technical cooperation, should promote the creation by each member country of a website targeted at SME users to provide easily accessible information on the Agreement and how they can use it for their advantage.

Policy suggestion

In line with specific provisions of Chapter 14 – Small and Medium Enterprises, SMEs in developing countries, especially in less developed economies, should be given assistance in the following priority areas: promoting the use of electronic commerce; promoting awareness, understanding, and effective use of the intellectual property system; and sharing best practices on enhancing SMEs' capability and competitiveness.

Economic and Technical Cooperation

Incremental value

Member countries are requested to undertake economic and technical cooperation activities, which are either trade- or investment-related, including capacity building and technical assistance focusing on (i) trade in goods, (ii) trade in services, (iii) investment, (iv) intellectual property, (v) electronic commerce, (vi) competition, and (vii) small and medium-sized enterprises.

Implementation and policy suggestion

The Agreement calls for development of a work program, under the Committee on Sustainable Development, which takes into account needs identified in various RCEP committees. The committee should consider (i) extending the illustrative sectoral coverage of the work program to include customs procedures and trade facilitation and procurement; and (ii) including in the work program not only capacity building and technical assistance and economic infrastructure and building productive capacity, which are fundamental for boosting trade capacity.

Procurement

Incremental value

The modest provision helps seven RCEP members that have not joined CPTPP nor WTO's Government Procurement Agreement (GPA) (Cambodia, the PRC, Indonesia, the Lao PDR, Myanmar, the Philippines, and Thailand) to understand the issue and prepare for going forward.

Built-in agenda

The chapter should be reviewed every 5 years. GPA provisions, rather than CPTPP, appear more in consonance with future amendments of the chapter.

Policy suggestion

Although least developed countries are exempt from all procurement obligations, they could benefit from capacity building and technical assistance in this area.

I   Comparison between CPTPP and RCEP

Table A.1.1: Australia

CPTPP (by staging category)	RCEP Staging Category	Frequency	%
(a) Category EIF: duties eliminated entirely from date of entry into force	A1 - Ad valorem tariffs reducing to 0 upon entry into force	1,711	27.67
	A3 - Ad valorem tariffs reducing at a constant rate until 0 in year 3	295	4.77
(b) Category AU3-A: duties immediately reduced to 2%, reduced to 1% in Year 2 and duty-free from Year 3	A7 - Ad valorem tariffs reducing at a constant rate until 0 in year 7	307	4.96
	A10 - Ad valorem tariffs reducing at a constant rate until 0 in year 10	306	4.95
(c) Category AU3-B: duties immediately reduced to 5%; duties eliminated from Year 3	A15 - Ad valorem tariffs reducing at a constant rate until 0 in year 15	120	1.94
(d) Category AU3-C: duties remain at base rate, duties eliminated from Year 3	A20 - Ad valorem tariffs reducing at a constant rate until 0 in year 20	380	6.14
	AB10 - Ad valorem tariffs reducing at a constant rate until a positive minimum rate in year 10	2	0.03
(e) Category B4: duties eliminated in four annual stages; duties eliminated from Year 4	C7 - A combination of Ad valorem and specific tariffs, reducing at a constant rate until 0 in year 7	2	0.03
		8	0.13
(f) Category AU4-A: duties reduced to 5%; duties eliminated from Year 4	C20 - A combination of Ad valorem and specific tariffs, reducing at a constant rate until 0 in year 20	2,943	47.59
		5	0.08
(g) Category AU4-B: duties remain at base rate, duties eliminated from Year 4	O - No tariff reduction, tariffs are 0		
	S1 - Specific tariffs, reducing to 0 upon entry into force	105	1.70
(h) Category AU-R1: the ad valorem component eliminated on the date of entry into force; non-ad valorem component shall be maintained	U - No tariff reduction		
	Total	**6,184**	**100.00**

CPTPP = Comprehensive and Progressive Agreement for Trans-Pacific Partnership, EIF = entry into force, RCEP = Regional Comprehensive Economic Partnership.
Tariff codes: A = Ad valorem tariff, S = Specific tariff, C = Combination of ad valorem and specific tariffs, TRQ = in-quota and out-quota tariffs, CKD = Complete knock down tariff rate imposed by Viet Nam.
Notes: Ax = Ad valorem tariff to be reduced at a constant rate to zero after x year(s); ABx = Ad valorem tariff to be reduced at a constant rate to a positive minimum tariff in x year(s); A1-TRQ = Ad valorem in-quota and out-quota tariffs to be reduced at a constant rate to zero upon entry into force; ABx-TRQ = Ad valorem in-quota and out-quota tariffs to be reduced at a constant rate to a positive minimum tariff in x year(s); Sx = Specific tariff to be reduced at a constant rate to zero after in x year(s); SBx = Specific tariff to be reduced at a constant rate to a positive minimum tariff in x year(s); Cx = Combination of ad valorem and specific tariffs to be reduced at a constant rate to zero after x year(s); CBx = Combination of ad valorem and specific tariffs to be reduced at a constant rate to a positive minimum tariff after x year(s); O = Non-dutiable goods (i.e., tariffs are zero); U = Excluded from any tariff reduction or elimination; U-TRQ = No tariff reduction for both in-quota tariffs and out-quota tariffs.
Source: Author representation based on official RCEP tariff schedules.

Table A.1.2: Brunei Darussalam

CPTPP (by staging category)	RCEP		
	Staging Category	Frequency	%
(a) Category EIF: duties eliminated entirely from the date of entry into force	A1 – Ad valorem tariffs reducing to 0 upon entry into force	29	0.29
b) Category BD3: duties remain at base rate; duties eliminated from Year 3	A10 – Ad valorem tariffs reducing at a constant rate until 0 in year 10	786	7.92
(c) Category BD6: duties remain at base rate; duties reduced to 15% ad valorem from Year 4; duties eliminated from Year 6	A15 – Ad valorem tariffs reducing at a constant rate until 0 in year 15	794	8.00
	A20 – Ad valorem tariffs reducing at a constant rate until 0 in year 20	536	5.40
(d) Category BD7-A: duties remain at base rate; duties eliminated from Year 7	AB18 – Ad valorem tariffs, reducing at a constant rate until a positive minimum rate in year 18	2	0.02
(e) Category BD7-B: duties remain at base rate; duties reduced to 10% ad valorem from Year 4 duties eliminated from Year 7	AB20 – Ad valorem tariffs, reducing at a constant rate until a positive minimum rate in year 20	4	0.04
	AB24 – Ad valorem tariffs, reducing at a constant rate until a positive minimum rate in year 24	34	0.34
(f) Category BD7-C: duties remain at base rate; duties reduced to 15% ad valorem from Year 4, 10% ad valorem from Year 6; duties from Year 7	O – No tariff reduction, tariffs are 0	7,568	76.22
	S15 – Specific tariffs, reducing at a constant rate until 0 in year 15	7	0.07
(g) Category BD7-D: duties remain at base rate; duties reduced to 5c/kg from Year 6; duties eliminated from Year 7	SB18 – Specific tariffs, reducing at a constant rate until a positive minimum rate in year 18	8	0.08
		25	0.25
(h) Category BD7-E: duties remain at base rate; duties reduced to 10c/kg from Year 6; duties eliminated from Year 7	SB20 – Specific tariffs, reducing at a constant rate until a positive minimum rate in year 20	136	1.37
(i) Category BD7-F: duties remain at base rate; duties reduced to 10c/dal from Year 6; duties eliminated from Year 7	U – No tariff reduction		
(j) Category BD7-G: duties remain at base rate; duties reduced to 20c/dal from Year 6; duties from Year 7			
(k) Category BD11: duties remain at base rate; duties eliminated from Year 11			
(l) Category BD-A: duties remain duty free on the date of entry into force; the import licensing and import restrictions on these goods shall remain			
	Total	9,929	100.00

CPTPP = Comprehensive and Progressive Agreement for Trans-Pacific Partnership, EIF = entry into force, RCEP = Regional Comprehensive Economic Partnership.
Source: Authors' representation based on official RCEP tariff schedules.

Table A.1.3: Japan

CPTPP (by staging category)	RCEP						
	Staging Category	ASEAN	Australia	PRC	Korea, Rep. of	New Zealand	Total
(a) Category EIF: duties eliminated entirely from date of entry into force.	A1 – Ad valorem tariffs, reducing to 0 upon entry into force	2,953	2,953	1,456	2,085	2,953	12,400
(b) Category JPEIF*: duties eliminated entirely on the date of entry into force besides levy; levy determined by tariff line	A11 – Ad valorem tariffs, reducing at a constant rate until 0 in year 11	450	450	1,443	763	450	3,556
(c) Category B4: duties eliminated in four annual stages, duties eliminated from April 1 of Year 4	A16 – Ad valorem tariffs, reducing at a constant rate until 0 in year 16	821	821	1,044	769	821	4,276
(d) Category B6: duties eliminated in six annual stages, duties eliminated from April 1 of Year 6	A21 – Ad valorem tariffs, reducing at a constant rate until 0 in year 21	1	1	93	1	1	97
(e)–(i) Category JPB6*, JPB6**, JPB6***, JPB6****, JPB6*****: duties eliminated by various percentages and annual stages	AB1 – Ad valorem tariffs, reducing to a positive rate upon entry into force (i.e., MFN tariff is higher than the tariff rate under RCEP)	52	52	0	0	52	156
(j) Category B8: duties eliminated in eight annual stages, duties eliminated from April 1 of Year 8	AB11 – Ad valorem tariffs, reducing at a constant rate until a positive minimum rate in year 11	1	1	0	0	1	3
(k) Category JPB8*, JPB8**, JPB8***, JPB8****, JPB8*****: duties eliminated by various annual stages and percentages and/or ad valorem rates	AB16 – Ad valorem tariffs, reducing at a constant rate until a positive minimum rate in year 16	0	0	0	52	0	52
(l) Category B9 (and B11): duties eliminated in nine (or eleven) annual stages; duties eliminated from April 1 of Year 9 (or Year 11)	C11 – A combination of ad valorem and specific tariffs, reducing at a constant rate until 0 in year 11	1	1	186	1	1	190
(m) Category JPB10*, JPB11*, JPB11**, JPB11***, JPB11****, JPB11****, JPB12*, JPB13*, JPB13**, JPB13***: duties eliminated by various ad valorem percentages and different annual stages	C16 – A combination of ad valorem and specific tariffs, reducing at a constant rate until 0 in year 16	32	32	35	18	32	149

continued on the next page

Table A.1.3 *continued*

CPTPP (by staging category)	Staging Category	RCEP					
		ASEAN	Australia	PRC	Korea, Rep. of	New Zealand	Total
(n) Category B16: duties eliminated in 16 annual stages; duties eliminated from April 1 of Year 16	CB1 - A combination of ad valorem and specific tariffs, reducing to a positive rate upon entry into force	1	1	0	0	1	3
(o) Category JPB16*, JPB16**, JPB16***, JPB16****, JPB21*, JPB21**, JPB21***, JPR2, JPR3, JPR4, JPR5, JPR6, JPR7, JPR8, JPR9, JPR10, JPR11, JPR12, JPR13, JPR14, JPR15, JPR16, JPR17 JPR18, JPR19, JPR20, JPR21, JPR22, JPR23, JPR24, JPR25: duties eliminated by weight and/or percentage through various annual stages and different schedules	O - No tariff reduction, tariffs are 0	3,684	3,684	3,684	3,684	3,684	18,420
	S1 - Specific tariffs, reducing to 0 upon entry into force	25	25	7	7	25	89
	S11 - Specific tariffs, reducing at a constant rate until 0 in year 11	27	27	12	12	27	105
	S16 - Specific tariffs, reducing at a constant rate until 0 in year 16	18	18	28	5	18	87
(p) Category JPM1, JPM2: determination of duties and elimination schedule is based on WTO agreement	S21 - Specific tariffs, reducing at a constant rate until 0 in year 21	1	1	1	1	1	5
(q) Category TRQ: duties governed by the terms of TRQ applicable to that tariff item (see Appendix A)	SB1 - Specific tariffs, reducing to a positive rate upon entry into force	2	2	0	0	2	6
(r) Category MFN: duties shall be Most-Favored-Nation rate at the time of import	SB11 - Specific tariffs, reducing at a constant rate until a positive minimum rate in year 11	1	1	0	0	1	3
	U - No tariff reduction	1,083	1,083	1,356	1,707	1,083	6,312
	Total	**9,381**	**9,381**	**9,381**	**9,326**	**9,381**	**46,850**

ASEAN = Association of Southeast Asian Nations, CPTPP = Comprehensive and Progressive Agreement for Trans-Pacific Partnership, EIF = entry into force, MFN = most favored nation, PRC = People's Republic of China, RCEP = Regional Comprehensive Economic Partnership, WTO = World Trade Organization.
Note: The base rates of duty set out in this Schedule reflect Japan's Most-Favored-Nation (MFN) rates of duty in effect on January 1, 2010, except for items identified by an asterisk (*) adjacent to the base rate. For these items, the applicable base rates of duty are otherwise indicated in this Schedule.
Source: Authors' representation based on official RCEP tariff schedules.

Table A.1.4: Malaysia

CPTPP (by staging category)	RCEP		
	Staging Category	**Frequency**	**%**
(a) Category EIF: duties eliminated entirely from date of entry into force	A1 – Ad valorem tariffs, reducing to 0 upon entry into force	503	5.34
(b) Category B3: duties eliminated in three annual stages; duties eliminated from Year 3	A10 – Ad valorem tariffs, reducing at a constant rate until 0 in year 10	1,250	13.26
	A15 – Ad valorem tariffs, reducing at a constant rate until 0 in year 15	573	6.08
(c) Category B6: duties eliminated in six annual stages; duties eliminated from Year 6	A20 – Ad valorem tariffs, reducing at a constant rate until 0 in year 20	69	0.73
(d) Category B8: duties eliminated in eight annual stages; duties eliminated from Year 8	AB23 – Ad valorem tariffs, reducing at a constant rate until a positive minimum rate in year 23	250	2.65
(e) Category B11: duties eliminated in 11 annual stages; duties eliminated from Year 11	C1 – A combination of ad valorem and specific tariffs, reducing to 0 upon entry into force.	1	0.01
(f) Category B13: duties eliminated in 13 annual stages; duties eliminated from Year 13	C10 – A combination of Ad valorem and specific tariffs, reducing at a constant rate until 0 in year 10	2	0.02
(g) Category B16: duties eliminated in 16 annual stages; duties eliminated from Year 16	O – No tariff reduction, tariffs are 0	6,086	64.57
	TRQ – Tariff rate quota, there is neither information on whether there is a tariff reduction or not nor information on tariff values	2	0.02
(h) Category TRQ: duties governed by the terms of the TRQ applicable to that tariff item (see Appendix A)	U – No tariff reduction	670	7.11
	U* – No tariff reduction, but base rate is a specific tariff while RCEP tariff is an ad valorem tariff	1	0.01
	U-TRQ – No tariff reduction for both in-quota tariffs and out-quota tariffs	18	0.19
	Total	**9,425**	**100.00**

CPTPP = Comprehensive and Progressive Agreement for Trans-Pacific Partnership, EIF = entry into force, RCEP = Regional Comprehensive Economic Partnership.
Source:Authors' representation based on official RCEP tariff schedules.

Table A.1.5: New Zealand

CPTPP (by staging category)	RCEP		
	Staging Category	Frequency	%
(a) Category EIF: duties eliminated entirely from date of entry into force	A1 - Ad valorem tariffs, reducing to 0 upon entry into force	512	6.85
(b) Category B2: duties eliminated in two annual stages, duties eliminated from Year 2	A10 - Ad valorem tariffs, reducing at a constant rate until 0 in year 10	1,186	15.86
(c) Category B5: duties eliminated in five annual stages; duties eliminated from Year 5	A15 - Ad valorem tariffs, reducing at a constant rate until 0 in year 15	781	10.44
	AB11 - Ad valorem tariffs, reducing at a constant rate until a positive minimum rate in year 11	370	4.95
(d) Category B7: duties eliminated in seven annual stages; duties eliminated from Year 7	AB16 - Ad valorem tariffs, reducing at a constant rate until a positive minimum rate in year 16	66	0.88
(e) Category NZ-Parts: duties receive the same tariff treatment as goods provided for in the corresponding non-parts tariff items	O - No tariff reduction, tariffs are 0	4,381	58.59
	S1 - Specific tariffs, reducing to 0 upon entry into force	1	0.01
	S10 - Specific tariffs, reducing at a constant rate until 0 in year 10	2	0.03
	S15 - Specific tariffs, reducing at a constant rate until 0 in year 15	3	0.04
	U - No tariff reduction	176	2.35
	Total	**7,478**	**100.00**

CPTPP = Comprehensive and Progressive Agreement for Trans-Pacific Partnership, EIF = entry into force, RCEP = Regional Comprehensive Economic Partnership.
Source: Authors' representation based on official RCEP tariff schedules.

Table A.1.6: Singapore

CPTPP (by staging category)	RCEP		
	Staging Category	Frequency	%
Category EIF: duties eliminated entirely from date of entry into force	O - No tariff reduction, tariffs are 0	9,552	99.94
	S1 - Specific tariffs, reducing to 0 upon entry into force	6	0.06
	Total	**9,558**	**100.00**

CPTPP = Comprehensive and Progressive Agreement for Trans-Pacific Partnership, EIF = entry into force, RCEP = Regional Comprehensive Economic Partnership.
Source: Authors' representation based on official RCEP tariff schedules.

Table A.1.7: Viet Nam

CPTPP (by staging category)	RCEP							
	Staging Category	ASEAN	Australia	PRC	Japan	Korea, Rep. of	New Zealand	Total
(a) Category EIF: duties eliminated entirely from the date of entry into force	A1 - Ad valorem tariffs, reducing to 0 upon entry into force	3,242	3,242	3,242	3,242	3,242	3,242	19,452
(b) Category B2: duties eliminated in two annual stages; duties eliminated from Year 2	A10 - Ad valorem tariffs, reducing at a constant rate until 0 in year 10	1,661	1,661	1,661	0	1,661	1,661	8,305
(c) Category B3: duties eliminated in three annual stages; duties eliminated from Year 3	A11 - Ad valorem tariffs, reducing at a constant rate until 0 in year 11	0	0	0	1,661	0	0	1,661
(d) Category B4: duties eliminated in four annual stages; duties eliminated from Year 4	A15 - Ad valorem tariffs, reducing at a constant rate until 0 in year 15	662	662	0	0	381	662	2367
(e) Category B5: duties eliminated in five annual stages; duties eliminated from Year 5	A16 - Ad valorem tariffs, reducing at a constant rate until 0 in year 16	0	0	0	381	0	0	381
(f) Category B6: duties shall be eliminated in six annual stages; duties eliminated from year 6	A20 - Ad valorem tariffs, reducing at a constant rate until 0 in year 20	65	0	281	0	0	0	346
eliminated from Year 8	AB20 - Ad valorem tariffs, reducing at a constant rate until a positive minimum rate in year 20	141	206	213	252	25	206	1,270
(g) Category B7: duties eliminated in seven annual stages, duties eliminated from Year 7	AB25 - Ad valorem tariffs, reducing at a constant rate until a positive minimum rate in year 25	126	126	109	288	288	126	1,063
(h) Category B8: duties eliminated in eight annual stages; duties eliminated from Year 8	CKD - The complete knock down (CKD) tariff rate imposed by Viet Nam, usually for the imported parts in complete sets for assembly into complete automobiles	87	87	87	87	87	87	522
(i) Category B10: duties eliminated in 10 annual stages; duties eliminated from Year 10 (j) Category B11: duties eliminated in 11 annual stages; duties eliminated from Year 11 (k) Category B12: duties eliminated in 12 annual stages; duties eliminated from Year 12	O - No tariff reduction, tariffs are 0	3,000	3,000	3,000	3,000	3,000	3,000	18,000

continued on the next page

Table A.1.7 *continued*

CPTPP (by staging category)	RCEP							
	Staging Category	ASEAN	Australia	PRC	Japan	Korea, Rep. of	New Zealand	Total
(l) Category B13: duties eliminated in 13 annual stages; duties eliminated from Year 13. (m) Category B16: duties eliminated in 16 annual stages; duties eliminated from Year 16. (n) Category VN4-A, VN4-B, VN7-A, VN8-A, VN8-B, VN10-A: duties reduced by ad valorem over various years before elimination. (o) Category VN11-A, VN11-B. VN11-C, VN11-D, VN11-E, VN11-F, VN11-G, VN11-H, VN11-I: depending on date of entry into force, duties reduced by ad valorem percentage at various annual stages and elimination schedules. (p) Category VN12-A, VN12-B, VN13-A, VN13-B, VN13-C, VN13-D, VN13-E, VN16-A, VN21-A: duties reduced by ad valorem percentage at various annual stages and elimination schedules. (q) Category TRQ (TRQ-VN1, TRQ-VN2 and TRQ-VN3): duties governed by the terms of the TRQ applicable to that tariff item, as outlined (r) Category VN22: base rate.	TRQ - Tariff rate quota, there is neither information on whether there is a tariff reduction or not nor information on tariff values.	30	30	30	30	30	30	180
	U - No tariff reduction.	544	544	935	617	617	544	3,801
	Total	**9,558**	**9,558**	**9,558**	**9,558**	**9,558**	**9,558**	**57,348**

ASEAN = Association of Southeast Asian Nations, CPTPP = Comprehensive and Progressive Agreement for Trans-Pacific Partnership, EIF = entry into force, PRC = People's Republic of China, RCEP = Regional Comprehensive Economic Partnership.
Source: Authors' representation based on official RCEP tariff schedules.

II – Countries with only RCEP

Table A.2.1: Cambodia

Staging Category	Frequency	%
A1 – Ad valorem tariffs, reducing to 0 upon entry into force.	1,566	16.38
A13 – Ad valorem tariffs, reducing at a constant rate until 0 in year 13.	2,868	30.01
A15 – Ad valorem tariffs, reducing at a constant rate until 0 in year 15.	1,969	20.60
A20 – Ad valorem tariffs, reducing at a constant rate until 0 in year 20.	623	6.52
C20 – A combination of ad valorem and specific tariffs, reducing at a constant rate until 0 in year 20.	5	0.05
O – No tariff reduction, tariffs are 0.	1,289	13.49
S20 – Specific tariffs, reducing at a constant rate until 0 in year 20.	2	0.02
U – No tariff reduction.	1,236	12.93
Total	**9,558**	**100.00**

Source: Authors' representation based on official Regional Comprehensive Economic Partnership tariff schedules.

Table A.2.2: People's Republic of China

Staging Category	ASEAN	Australia	Japan	Korea, Rep. of	New Zealand	Total
A1 – Ad valorem tariffs, reducing to 0 upon entry into force	4,922	4,749	1,371	2,499	4,775	18,316
A10 – Ad valorem tariffs, reducing at a constant rate until 0 in year 10	1,052	1,173	0	3,397	1,148	6,770
A11 – Ad valorem tariffs, reducing at a constant rate until 0 in year 11	0	0	3,848	0	0	3,848
A15 – Ad valorem tariffs, reducing at a constant rate until 0 in year 15	248	0	0	255	0	503
A16 – Ad valorem tariffs, reducing at a constant rate until 0 in year 16	0	0	952	0	0	952
A20 – Ad valorem tariffs, reducing at a constant rate until 0 in year 20	570	827	0	268	826	2,491
A21 – Ad valorem tariffs, reducing at a constant rate until 0 in year 21	0	0	248	0	0	248
AB1 – Ad valorem tariffs, reducing to a positive rate upon entry into force (i.e., MFN tariff is higher than the tariff rate under RCEP)	361	355	30	3	356	1,105
AB10 – Ad valorem tariffs, reducing at a constant rate until a positive minimum rate in year 10	82	102	0	0	109	293
AB33 – Ad valorem tariffs, reducing at a constant rate until a positive minimum rate in year 33	0	0	0	1	0	1
AB34 – Ad valorem tariffs, reducing at a constant rate until a positive minimum rate in year 34	0	0	0	2	0	2
AB35 – Ad valorem tariffs, reducing at a constant rate until a positive minimum rate in year 35	0	0	0	78	0	78

continued on the next page

Table A.2.2 *continued*

Staging Category	ASEAN	Australia	Japan	Korea, Rep. of	New Zealand	Total
AB9 – Ad valorem tariffs, reducing at a constant rate until a positive minimum rate in year 9	3	3	0	0	3	9
O – No tariff reduction, tariffs are 0	699	699	699	699	699	3,495
U – No tariff reduction	340	369	1,129	1,075	361	3,274
Total	**8,277**	**8,277**	**8,277**	**8,277**	**8,277**	**41,385**

ASEAN = Association of Southeast Asian Nations, MFN = most favored nation, RCEP = Regional Comprehensive Economic Partnership.
Source: Authors' representation based on official RCEP tariff schedules.

Table A.2.3: Indonesia

Staging Category	ASEAN	Australia	PRC	Japan	Korea, Rep. of	New Zealand	Total
A1 – Ad valorem tariffs, reducing to 0 upon entry into force	5,269	5,264	5,263	5,269	5,255	5,264	31,584
A5 – Ad valorem tariffs, reducing at a constant rate until 0 in year 5	0	0	0	0	0	1	1
A10 – Ad valorem tariffs, reducing at a constant rate until 0 in year 10	1,581	1,515	1,508	1,509	1,518	1,579	9,210
A15 – Ad valorem tariffs, reducing at a constant rate until 0 in year 15	975	920	740	799	694	923	5,051
A20 – Ad valorem tariffs, reducing at a constant rate until 0 in year 20	126	135	192	126	236	137	952
AB18 – Ad valorem tariffs, reducing at a constant rate until a positive minimum rate in year 18	0	0	4	1	1	0	6
AB20 – Ad valorem tariffs, reducing at a constant rate until a positive minimum rate in year 20	0	0	1	327	301	2	631
AB23 – Ad valorem tariffs, reducing at a constant rate until a positive minimum rate in year 23	372	342	260	6	6	340	1,326
O – No tariff reduction, tariffs are 0	1,251	1,251	1,250	1,250	1,250	1,251	7,503
S1 – Specific tariffs, reducing to 0 upon entry into force	2	2	2	2	2	2	12
S20 – Specific tariffs, reducing at a constant rate until 0 in year 20	4	4	4	4	4	4	24
U – No tariff reduction	414	561	770	701	727	491	3,664
U* – No tariff reduction, but base rate is a specific tariff while RCEP tariff is an ad valorem tariff	18	18	18	18	18	18	108
Total	**10,012**	**10,012**	**10,012**	**10,012**	**10,012**	**10,012**	**60,072**

ASEAN = Association of Southeast Asian Nations, PRC = People's Republic of China, RCEP = Regional Comprehensive Economic Partnership.
Source: Taxonomy and calculation elaborated by the authors based on official RCEP tariff schedules

Table A.2.4: Lao People's Democratic Republic

Staging Category	Frequency	%
A1 – Ad valorem tariffs, reducing to 0 upon entry into force	2,858	29.90
A13 – Ad valorem tariffs, reducing at a constant rate until 0 in year 13	2,872	30.05
A15 – Ad valorem tariffs, reducing at a constant rate until 0 in year 15	1,895	19.83
A20 – Ad valorem tariffs, reducing at a constant rate until 0 in year 20	594	6.21
U – No tariff reduction	1,339	14.01
Total	**9,558**	**100.00**

Source: Authors' representation based on official Regional Comprehensive Economic Partnership tariff schedules.

Table A.2.5: Myanmar

Staging Category	Frequency	%
A1 – Ad valorem tariffs, reducing to 0 upon entry into force	2,533	25.79
A13 – Ad valorem tariffs, reducing at a constant rate until 0 in year 13	2,947	30.01
A15 – Ad valorem tariffs, reducing at a constant rate until 0 in year 15	1,964	20.00
A20 – Ad valorem tariffs, reducing at a constant rate until 0 in year 20	590	6.01
O – No tariff reduction, tariffs are 0	416	4.24
U – No tariff reduction	1,371	13.96
Total	**9,821**	**100.00**

Source: Authors' representation based on official Regional Comprehensive Economic Partnership tariff schedules.

Table A.2.6: Philippines

Staging Category	ASEAN	Australia/ New Zealand	PRC	Japan	Korea, Rep. of	Total
A1 - Ad valorem tariffs, reducing to 0 upon entry into force	7,571	7,565	7,469	7,565	7,536	37,706
A1-TRQ - There are ad valorem in-quota tariff rates and ad valorem out-quota tariff rates, reducing to 0 upon entry into force	8	8	8	8	8	40
A15 - ad valorem tariffs, reducing at a constant rate until 0 in year 15	860	866	962	862	844	4,394
A20 - ad valorem tariffs, reducing at a constant rate until 0 in year 20	45	45	45	45	45	225
AB11 -ad valorem tariffs, reducing at a constant rate until a positive minimum rate in year 11	52	52	52	52	52	260
AB12-TRQ - There are ad valorem in-quota tariff rates and ad valorem out-quota tariff rates, reducing at a constant rate until a positive minimum rate in year 12	3	3	3	3	3	15
AB15 ad valorem tariffs, reducing at a constant rate until a positive minimum rate in year 15	340	340	334	340	340	1,694
AB15-TRQ - There are ad valorem in-quota tariff rates and ad valorem out-quota tariff rates, reducing at a constant rate until a positive minimum rate in year 15	6	6	5	6	6	29
AB16 -ad valorem tariffs, reducing at a constant rate until a positive minimum rate in year 16	2	2	2	2	2	10
AB20 - ad valorem tariffs, reducing at a constant rate until a positive minimum rate in year 20	191	191	190	191	191	954
AB20-TRQ - There are ad valorem in-quota tariff rates and ad valorem out-quota tariff rates, reducing at a constant rate until a positive minimum rate in year 20	13	13	7	13	13	59
O - No tariff reduction, tariffs are 0	477	477	477	477	477	2,385
U - No tariff reduction	106	106	121	110	157	600
U-TRQ-M - No tariff reduction for both in-quota tariffs and out-quota tariffs, and no information on the values of tariffs	48	48	48	48	48	240
Total	9,722	9,722	9,723	9,722	9,722	48,611

ASEAN = Association of Southeast Asian Nations, MFN = most favored nation, PRC = People's Republic of China, RCEP = Regional Comprehensive Economic Partnership.
Source: Authors' representation based on official RCEP tariff schedules.

Table A.2.7: Republic of Korea

Staging Category	ASEAN	Australia	PRC	Japan	New Zealand	Total
A1 – Ad valorem tariffs, reducing to 0 upon entry into force	5,857	5,854	4,180	3,084	5,856	24,831
A10 – Ad valorem tariffs, reducing at a constant rate until 0 in year 10	1,962	1,961	3,290	3,959	1,962	13,134
A15 – Ad valorem tariffs, reducing at a constant rate until 0 in year 15	1,209	1,209	1,042	669	1,209	5,338
A20 – Ad valorem tariffs, reducing at a constant rate until 0 in year 20	79	61	20	455	67	682
AB1 – Ad valorem tariffs, reducing to a positive rate upon entry into force (i.e., MFN tariff is higher than the tariff rate under RCEP)	5	0	8	0	0	13
AB18 – Ad valorem tariffs, reducing at a constant rate until a positive minimum rate in year 18	5	5	0	0	5	15
AB19 – Ad valorem tariffs, reducing at a constant rate until a positive minimum rate in year 19	9	9	0	0	9	27
AB20 – Ad valorem tariffs, reducing at a constant rate until a positive minimum rate in year 20	490	485	0	0	485	1,460
AB33 – Ad valorem tariffs, reducing at a constant rate until a positive minimum rate in year 33	0	0	2	0	0	2
AB34 – Ad valorem tariffs, reducing at a constant rate until a positive minimum rate in year 34	0	0	33	0	0	33
AB35 – Ad valorem tariffs, reducing at a constant rate until a positive minimum rate in year 35	0	0	88	0	0	88
C1 – A combination of ad valorem and specific tariffs, reducing to 0 upon entry into force	29	29	29	29	29	145
C10 – A combination of Ad valorem and specific tariffs, reducing at a constant rate until 0 in year 10	5	5	5	6	5	26
C15 – A combination of Ad valorem and specific tariffs, reducing at a constant rate until 0 in year 15	6	6	6	0	6	24
C20 – A combination of Ad valorem and specific tariffs, reducing at a constant rate until 0 in year 20	1	1	0	0	1	3
CB20 – A combination of Ad valorem and specific tariffs, reducing at a constant rate until a positive minimum rate in year 20	2	2	0	0	2	6
O – No tariff reduction, tariffs are 0	1,956	1,956	1,956	1,956	1,956	9,780
S1 – Specific tariffs, reducing to 0 upon entry into force	1	1	1	0	1	4
S1 – Specific tariffs, reducing to 0 upon entry into force	0	0	0	1	0	1
U – No tariff reduction	628	659	1,584	2,085	651	5,607
Total	**12,244**	**12,243**	**12,244**	**12,243**	**12,244**	**61,218**

ASEAN = Association of Southeast Asian Nations, MFN = most favored nation, PRC = People's Republic of China, RCEP = Regional Comprehensive Economic Partnership.
Source: Taxonomy and calculation elaborated by the authors based on official RCEP tariff schedules.

Table A.2.8: Thailand

Staging Category	Frequency	%
A1 - Ad valorem tariffs, reducing at a constant rate until 0 in year 10	4,612	48.25
A10 - Ad valorem tariffs, reducing at a constant rate until 0 in year 10	1,281	13.40
A15 - Ad valorem tariffs, reducing at a constant rate until 0 in year 15	852	8.91
A20 - Ad valorem tariffs, reducing at a constant rate until 0 in year 20	246	2.57
AB20 - Ad valorem tariffs, reducing at a constant rate until a positive minimum rate in year 20	115	1.20
O - No tariff reduction, tariffs are 0	1,694	17.72
S1 - Specific tariffs, reducing to 0 upon entry into force	34	0.36
S10 - Specific tariffs, reducing at a constant rate until 0 in year 10	1	0.01
S20 - Specific tariffs, reducing at a constant rate until 0 in year 20	4	0.04
U - No tariff reduction	719	7.52
Total	**9,558**	**100.00**

Source: Authors' representation based on official Regional Comprehensive Economic Partnership tariff schedules.

III Countries with only CPTPP

Table A.3.1: Countries with Comprehensive and Progressive Agreement for Trans-Pacific Partnership Agreements

	Staging Category
Canada	(a) Category EIF: duties eliminated entirely from the date of entry into force.
	(b) Category B4: duties eliminated in four annual stages; duties eliminated Year 4.
	(c) Category B6: duties eliminated in six annual stages; duties eliminated from Year 6.
	(d) Category B7: duties eliminated in seven annual stages; duties eliminated from Year 7.
	(e) Category B11: duties eliminated in 11 annual stages, duties eliminated from Year 11.
	(f) Category CA1: duties maintained at base rate Years 1–8; duties eliminated in four annual stages beginning Year 9, duties eliminated from Year 12.
	(g) Category CA2: duties reduced to one-quarter of base rate and maintained through Year 11; duties eliminated from Year 12.
	(h) Category CA3: duties reduced to 5.5%, 5.0%, 2.5%, 2.0% over Years 1–4; duties eliminated from Year 5.
	(i) Category TRQ: duties governed by the terms of the TRQ applicable to that tariff item (see Appendix A).
Chile	(a) Category EIF: duties eliminated entirely from the date of entry into force.
	(b) Category B4: duties eliminated in four annual stages; duties eliminated from Year 4.
	(c) Category B8: duties eliminated in eight annual stages; duties eliminated from Year 8.
	(d) Categories CL-AU FTA, CL-P4, CL-CA FTA, CL-JP SEP, CL-MY-CL-MX FTA, CL-PE FTA, CL-US FTA, CL-VN FTA; duties for Wheat and Sugar vary by previously established FTA.
	(e) Category CL-MFN: duties shall be the MFN rate.

continued on the next page

Table A.3.1 *continued*

	Staging Category
Mexico	(a) Category EIF: duties eliminated entirely from the date of entry into force. (b) Category B3: duties eliminated in three annual stages; duties eliminated from Year 3. (c) Category B5: duties eliminated in five annual stages, duties eliminated from Year 5. (d) Category B8: duties eliminated in eight annual stages; duties eliminated from Year 8. (e) Category B10: duties eliminated in 10 annual stages; duties eliminated from Year 10. (f) Category B12: duties eliminated in 12 annual stages; duties eliminated from Year 12. (g) Category B13: duties eliminated in 13 annual stages; duties eliminated from Year 13. (h) Category B15: duties shall be eliminated in 15 annual stages; duties eliminated from Year 15. (i) Category B16: duties eliminated in 16 annual stages; duties eliminated from Year 16. (j) Category D: rate of customs duty applied under the WTO Agreement. (k) Category MX10, MX11, MX13, MX16: duties maintained different rates before elimination through different annual stages. (l) Category MX-R1, MX-R2, MXR3: duties reduced by various annual stages and percentages. (m) Category MX-R4, MX-R5, MX-R6: duties reduced by various annual stages. (n) Category MX-R7: duties reduced to 47.5% in Year 1. (o) Category CSQ: duties governed by terms of the CSQ for that specific tariff line (see Appendix A). (p) Category CSA: duties governed by terms of the CSA for that specific tariff line (see Appendix A).
Peru	(a) Category EIF: duties eliminated entirely from the date of entry into force. (b) Category B6: duties eliminated in six annual stages, duties eliminated from Year 6. (c) Category B11: duties eliminated in 11 annual stages; duties eliminated from Year 11. (d) Category B13: duties eliminated in 13 annual stages, duties eliminated from Year 13. (e) Category B16: duties eliminated in 16 annual stages; duties eliminated from Year 16. (f) Category PE-R1, PE-R2: ad valorem duties reduced on different annual elimination schedules; specific duties from Peruvian Price Band System excluded.

Source: Authors' representation based on official Regional Comprehensive Economic Partnership tariff schedules.

References

Association of Southeast Asian Nations (ASEAN). 2021. A Recent Development of the Cambodia's Draft Law on Competition. *ASEAN Competition News Update.* 23 March. https://asean-competition.org/read-news-update-a-recent-development-of-the-cambodias-draft-law-on-competition.

Australia Department of Foreign Affairs and Trade (DFAT). 2020. RCEP—Outcomes: Services and Investment. Canberra. https://www.dfat.gov.au/sites/default/files/rcep-outcomes-services-and-investment.pdf.

Baker McKenzie. 2020. China: Impact of the Regional Comprehensive Economic Partnership on Intellectual Property Protection. *Lexology.* 11 December. https://www.lexology.com/library/detail.aspx?g=0e2b811e-33e3-42d3-a1a9-5f555d5508a9.

Basu Das, S. 2015a. Challenges in Negotiating the Regional Comprehensive Economic Partnership Agreement in *The ASEAN Economic Community and Beyond: Myths and Realities,* ISEAS-Yusof Ishak Institute.

Basu Das, S. 2015b. The Regional Comprehensive Economic Partnership: Going Beyond ASEAN+1 Countries with Comprehensive and Progressive Trans-Pacific Partnership Agreements *The ASEAN Economic Community and Beyond: Myths and Realities.* ISEAS-Yusof Ishak Institute.

Corcoran, A. and R. Gillanders. 2015. Foreign Direct Investment and the Ease of Doing Business. *Review of World Economics.* 151 (1). pp. 103–26.

Crawford, J. A. and B. Kotschwar. 2018. Investment Provisions in Preferential Trade Agreements: Evolution and Current Trends. *WTO Staff Working Paper.* ERSD-2018-14. Geneva: World Trade Organization. https://www.wto.org/english/res_e/reser_e/ersd201814_e.pdf.

Crivelli, P., J. Hugot, and R. Platitas. 2021. The Regional Comprehensive Economic Partnership: A Stepping-Stone Toward Deeper Market Integration in *Asian Development Outlook 2021: Financing a Green and Inclusive Recovery.* Manila: Asian Development Bank.

Crivelli, P. and S. Inama. 2021 . Making RCEP Successful Through Business-friendly Rules of Origin. *Asian Development Blog.* Manila. 12 February. https://blogs.adb.org/blog/making-rcep-successful-through-business-friendly-rules-origin.

Crivelli, P. and S. Inama. 2022a. A Preliminary Assessment of the Regional Comprehensive Economic Partnership. *ADB Briefs no. 206.* Manila: Asian Development Bank.

Crivelli, P. and S. Inama. 2022b. China's CPTPP Accession and Implications for ASEAN. *ASEANFocus.* 2022 (1). pp. 14–15. https://www.iseas.edu.sg/wp-content/uploads/2022/03/ASEANFocus-Mar-2022-Final-LR-V2.pdf.

Crivelli, P., S. Inama, and J. Kasteng. 2021. Using Utilization Rates to Identify Rules of Origin Reforms: The Case of EU Free Trade Area Agreements. San Domenico di Fiesole, Italy: European University Institute. https://cadmus.eui.eu/handle/1814/70396.

Crivelli, P., S. Inama, and M. Pearson. 2022. An Analysis of Product-Specific Rules of Origin of the Regional Comprehensive Economic Partnership. Manila: Asian Development Bank.

Elms, D. 2021. Getting RCEP across the Line. *World Trade Review*. 20 (3). pp. 373–80. doi:10.1017/S1474745620000592.

EU-ASEAN Business Council (EABC). 2019. *Non-Tariff Barriers (NTBs) in ASEAN and Their Elimination from a Business Perspective.* Singapore.

Ewing-Chow, M. and J.J. Losari. 2020. RCEP Investment Chapter—A State-to-State WTO Style System for Now. *Kluwer Arbitration Blog.* 8 December.

Financial Times. 2020. Asian Trade Deal Set to be Signed after Years of Negotiations. 17 November. https://www.ft.com/content/ddaa403a-099c-423c-a273-6a2ed6ef45f2 (paywall).

Freund, C. 2016. Other New Areas: Customs Administration and Trade Facilitation, Anticorruption, Small and Medium-sized Enterprises, and More. In J. J. Schott and C. Cimino-Isaacs, eds. *Assessing The Trans-Pacific Partnership.* Volume 2. Washington, DC: Peterson Institute for International Economics.

Gadbaw, R. M. 2016. Competition Policy. In J. J. Schott and C. Cimino-Isaacs, eds. *Assessing The Trans-Pacific Partnership.* Volume 2. Washington, DC: Peterson Institute for International Economics.

Gelpern, A. 2016. Financial Services: Assessing the Trans-Pacific Partnership.In J. J. Schott and C. Cimino-Isaacs, eds. *Assessing The Trans-Pacific Partnership*. Volume 1. Washington, DC: Peterson Institute for International Economics.

Goodman, M. P. 2018. From TPP to CPTPP. Washington, DC: Center for Strategic and International Studies. 8 March. https://www.csis.org/analysis/tpp-cptpp.

Gootiiz, B. and A. Mattoo. 2017. Services in the Trans-Pacific Partnership. What Would Be Lost? *Policy Research Working Paper.* No. 7964. Washington, DC: World Bank.

Hayakawa, K., S. Urata, and T. Yoshimi. 2020. Designing Megaregional Trade Agreements, VOX EU, 8 March 2020. https://voxeu.org/article/designing-mega-regional-trade-agreements.

Honey, S. 2021. Asia-Pacific Digital Trade Policy Innovation. In I. Borchert and L. Alan Winters, eds. *Addressing Impediments to Digital Trade.* Washington, DC: Center for Economic Policy Research. https://voxeu.org/article/addressing-impediments-digital-trade-new-ebook.

Hornok, C. and M. Koren. 2015. Administrative Barriers to Trade. *Journal of International Economics.* 96. Supp. 1. pp. S110–S122. www.sciencedirect.com/science/article/pii/S0022199615000033.

Inama, S. and E.W. Sim. 2015. *ASEAN Rules of Origin.* Cambridge, UK: Cambridge University Press.

Japan External Trade Organization (JETRO). 2004. ASEAN FTAs and Rules of Origin. Overseas Research Department. Bangkok: JETRO. https://www.jetro.go.jp/ext_images/thailand/e_survey/pdf/fta_rulesoforigin.pdf.

Kniahin, D. et al. 2019. *Global Landscape of Rules of Origin: Insights from the New Comprehensive Database. GTAP Conference Paper.* https://www.gtap.agecon.purdue.edu/resources/download/9488.pdf.

Neo, D., P. Sauvé, and I. Streho. 2019. *Services Trade in ASEAN.* Cambridge, UK: Cambridge University Press.

New Zealand Ministry of Foreign Affairs and Trade. 2020 (MFAT). *Regional Comprehensive Economic Partnership National Interest Analysis.* https://www.mfat.govt.nz/assets/Uploads/RCEP-National-Interest-Analysis.pdf.

_____. 2020. *RCEP—Summary of Outcomes.* Wellington. https://www.mfat.govt.nz/assets/Trade-agreements/RCEP/RECP-Agreement-112020/RCEP-Summary-of-Outcomes.pdf.

Nguyen, H. H. and Q.H. Truong. 2019. Vietnam and the CPTPP: Achievements and Challenges. ISEAS-Yusof Ishak Institute. *Perspective*. 41. https://www.iseas.edu.sg/images/pdf/ISEAS_Perspective_2019_41.pdf.

Park, C.Y., P. Petri, and M. Plummer. 2021. The Economics of Conflict and Cooperation in the Asia-Pacific: RCEP, CPTPP and the US-China Trade War. *East Asian Economic Review*. 25 (3). pp. 233–72. https://www.eaerweb.org/selectArticleInfo.do;jsessionid=688B3CA687284E6A54A917DCE8FDB9D0#T001.

Rashmi B., K. P. Gallagher, and G. Prerna Sharma. 2021. RCEP: Goods Market Access Implications for ASEAN. *Global Development Policy Center Working Paper*. 045, 03/2021. https://www.bu.edu/gdp/files/2021/03/GEGI_WP_045_FIN.pdf.

Tan, I. et al. 2020. *Understanding the Regional Comprehensive Economic Partnership Agreement (RCEP): What does the RCEP mean to businesses?*. https://www.bakermckenzie.com/-/media/files/insight/publications/2020/12/bakermckenzie_understandingrcep_dec2020.pdf?la=en

Tang, D. and S. Wei. 2020. Brief Comments on China's Commitments on the Foreign Investment Access under the RCEP. Han Kun Law Offices. *News and Insights*. 15 December. https://www.hankunlaw.com/downloadfile/newsAndInsights/4cbeea5e53234067290b7aaafc7963b0.pdf.

Trivedi, J. et al. 2019. Non-Tariff Measures in Regional Trade Agreements in Asia and the Pacific: SPS, TBT and Government Procurement. ESCAP Trade, Investment and Innovation Division. *Working Paper Series*. No. 3. Bangkok: UNESCAP.

United Nations Conference on Trade and Development (UNCTAD). 2017. Improving Investment Dispute Settlement: UNCTAD Policy Tools. *IIA Issues Note*. Issue 4. November. Geneva.

UNCTAD. 2020. *Global Investment Trends Monitor. Special Issue: RCEP Agreement*. November. Geneva.

UNCTAD. 2021. What is at Stake for Developing Countries in Trade Negotiations on E-commerce? The Case of the Joint Statement Initiative. Geneva.

United States International Trade Commission. 2016. *Trans-Pacific Partnership Agreement: Likely Impact on the US Economy and on Specific Industry Sectors*. Publication Number: 4607. May. https://www.usitc.gov/publications/332/pub4607.pdf.

World Bank. 2018. *Connecting to Compete 2018—Trade Logistics in the Global Economy*. Washington, DC.

World Bank. 2020. Doing Business 2020. Washington, DC: World Bank.

World Trade Organization. 2021. Trade Facilitation Agreement Database. https://tfadatabase.org/implementation.

_____. 2021a. Australia – Anti-Dumping and Countervailing Duty Measures on Certain Products from China. Request for Consultations by China. WT/DS603/1, G/L/1391 G/ADP/D138/1, G/SCM/D133/1. 29 June 2021.

_____. 2021b. China – Anti-Dumping and Countervailing Duty Measures on Wine from Australia. Request for Consultations by Australia. WT/DS602/1, G/L/1390 G/ADP/D137/1, G/SCM/D132/1. 28 June 2021.

_____. 2021c. China - Anti-Dumping Measures on Stainless Steel Products from Japan. Request for Consultations by Japan. WT/DS601/1 G/L/1389 G/ADP/D136/1. 15 June 2021.

Wu, C.H. 2019. ASEAN at the Crossroads: Trap and Track between CPTPP and RCEP. *Journal of International Economic Law*. 23 (1). pp. 97–117.

www.ingramcontent.com/pod-product-compliance
Lightning Source LLC
Chambersburg PA
CBHW042033220326
41599CB00045BA/7284